# What can I do with... a media studies degree?

*Margaret McAlpine*

*What can I do with... a media studies degree?*
This first edition published in 2003 by Trotman and Company Ltd
2 The Green, Richmond, Surrey TW9 1PL

© Trotman and Company Limited 2003

The HESA data quoted in this publication is from the HESA Student
Record July 2001; © Higher Education Statistics Agency Limited 2002.

The Higher Education Statistics Agency (HESA) does not accept any
responsibility for any references or conclusions derived from the
data quoted in this publication.

British Library Cataloguing in Publication Data
A catalogue record for this book is available from the British Library

ISBN 0 85660 866 1

Typeset by Mac Style Ltd, Scarborough, N. Yorkshire

Printed and bound in Great Britain by Creative Print and Design
(Wales) Ltd

# Contents

# About the author

Margaret McAlpine taught for a number of years in schools and colleges in the Midlands and East Anglia, before becoming a journalist. Today she writes for a variety of publications and has a particular interest in writing careers materials for young people. Her other titles published by Trotman are *What can I do with... no degree?* and *What can I do with... a law degree?*

She has three grown-up children and lives with her husband in Suffolk.

# Taking a
# Year Off

## Margaret Flynn

**A YEAR OUT** can give young people a valuable and challenging learning experience – provided it is carefully planned. The new edition of *Taking a Year Off* has been written to help those considering a gap year make the best use of their time, and examines all of the options available.

5th edition
085660 850 5
**£11.99**

# Introduction

The media is a powerful tool, affecting public opinion and attitudes on all sorts of issues. What's more its influence is increasing daily with the development of new technology.

The term 'media' covers a wide range of different communication systems: print (newspapers, magazines, books), radio, television, video, cinema and the fast-growing interactive media, which has grown out of the merging of computer and telecommunications technology with traditional communications systems.

Today most households in the UK own several televisions, the vast majority of cars have radios fitted, over 13 million people regularly read a newspaper and the Internet has become a major form of communication.

As the power of the media grows so does its fascination. Not only do people want to know how it works and why, they also want to work in an exciting, fast-moving industry.

One way into such work is by taking a media-related degree and there are over 2,000 such courses available across the UK. So how do you begin to select a course from such a bewildering array?

The choice is made even more difficult by the fact that while courses may have similar names they can vary from the almost completely practical to the purely academic. A lot of time and effort is needed to find the right course, and a good place to begin is Chapter 2 of this book.

Whatever your qualifications, finding a job in the media is difficult. There are more people chasing work than there are openings and a media-related degree can never be seen as a guarantee of a job. Getting that first foot in the door takes energy, determination and luck.

If your ambition is to work in the media, you need to be looking at courses that have strong links with the industry and which offer, as part of the course, job placements of at least a month. These placements provide hands-on experience that can never be found in lecture halls, plus a chance to make contacts and impress the people who matter. For further information and advice on work experience, see Chapter 3.

Not everyone who is interested in studying for a media-related degree wants to work in the industry. You don't have to be a camera operator to be interested in the development of the cinema.

Graduates with a degree in nursing, accountancy, physiotherapy or a similar career-related course usually have a clear work path ahead. Those who have studied academic subjects such as geography, history, archaeology or biology often use the skills they have gained during their studies in jobs that appear at first sight to be unrelated; this is also the case with media graduates.

They may never appear on television or behind a camera, but their careers owe a great deal to the qualities they developed during their media degree course.

## Practical, soft or transferable skills

These transferable skills do not relate to academic study but to more practical qualities, useful in a great many different situations. Once you have gained them they are with you for life and are greatly valued by employers.

Transferable skills gained from studying for a media degree include:

★ communication skills – the ability to explain what you mean simply and directly
★ creative skills – having an original and individual approach, seeing things in a new and interesting way
★ flexibility – the ability to adapt to changing situations
★ problem solving – looking for new ways to tackle issues and move forward
★ tenacity – sticking power
★ personal marketing skills – presenting yourself in the best and most positive light
★ technical skills – the ability to use a wide range of equipment such as computers, cameras, recording equipment and videos
★ team skills – working well as part of a group
★ organisational skills.

The following pages contain a number of profiles of young people either studying for a media-related degree, working in the media industry or in other job areas, all using the above skills in a variety of different ways.

# 1     Myths and facts

## Myth

### A media-related degree doesn't lead anywhere for most people

While many graduates have difficulty in finding work in the media industry, a significant proportion are successful.

Those who work in other areas take with them a wealth of qualities that make them very attractive to employers. With their excellent communication skills, media graduates enjoy careers in sales, retail, leisure and tourism, and many different areas of work.

## Myth

### A media-related degree is not as demanding as many other subjects

Reading through the profiles of young people with media-related degrees, the most valuable quality most frequently mentioned as being gained from their studies is the ability to organise a complicated and demanding workload.

Many degree courses combine both practical work and theory and this is a great introduction to the world of work, whatever that work may be.

## Myth

### You need a media degree for a media career

Studying for a degree means you gain a great deal of knowledge plus the transferable skills listed in the Introduction. However, it is no guarantee that you will find a job in the media industry.

Far more important than a degree is having the right type of personality. Determination is the major requirement. You need to be single minded, prepared to work unsociable hours, do any sort of job that is required and to move around the country at a moment's notice.

You have to be able to sell yourself and your abilities, write endless letters, make dozens of phone calls, follow up the smallest lead and recover from the disappointment you feel when you still don't seem to be getting anywhere.

## Myth

### A career in the media is exciting and glamorous

If you believe that a job in the media means rubbing shoulders with celebrities, being invited to film premieres and parties, you will be disappointed. It's more likely to mean getting up before dawn, arriving home after midnight, standing around in the cold and the rain and going without a lunch break because of a last minute hitch.

For the past six months Angharad has been up before daybreak. Her alarm rings at 4am and within minutes she is out of the door and on her way to the studios of independent radio station Red Dragon FM in Cardiff.

## Angharad Thomas
### Broadcast Journalist, Red Dragon FM Cardiff

**A-levels:** English, Psychology, Performing Arts
**Degree:** BA English Literature and Film, Sheffield Hallam University
**Postgraduate Diploma:** Broadcast Journalism, University of Central England, Birmingham

'I live close to the studio, so I just throw on my clothes and wake up when I get there. Sometimes I sleep in the afternoons or I have a very early night. It's a question of listening to your body and sleeping when you're tired.

'Work starts at 4.30am and I'm on my own in the newsroom until 10.30am. My job involves finding news stories, researching and writing them, deciding on the running order of news items and cutting them to fit time slots.

'As an independent radio station Red Dragon plays a lot of music and I interview a variety of different people, from musicians to politicians. I love the buzz and excitement of broadcast journalism.

'After leaving Sheffield Hallam I spent a month on a work placement with a local newspaper, the *Flintshire Chronicle*. At that time I was thinking of going into print journalism, but after work experience on BBC Radio Wales and on the independent radio station Heart FM, I decided broadcast journalism was for me.

'My first full-time job was with Beacon FM and from there I was invited to join Red Dragon. The unsociable hours don't bother me. I work with a great group of people and the fact that the work is unpredictable keeps me on my toes.

'I learnt at college that you can never take things for granted in broadcast journalism. A friend and I were running the news desk of the college radio. Nothing was happening and I remarked that I'd never known a more boring day. It was 11 September 2001 and we were minutes away from the news that shook the world.'

## Fact

### *Employers are not always impressed by media degrees*

An academic qualification is not the first thing employers in the media industry are looking for. They want enthusiastic, hard working young people who have a realistic idea of the work involved in a job. However, the skills and knowledge gained from taking a media-related degree can be a significant help in finding a job in the industry.

## Fact

### *There's less job security in the media industry than in other areas of work*

Today short-term contracts and freelance work are becoming the way forward for many people. The days of finding a job for life are almost certainly gone forever. Most people have a number of job changes during their careers.

However, jobs in the media are less secure than those in many other sectors, with a growing trend towards self-employment. A media career is not a good idea for anyone who hankers after security and a pension.

Hani Shawwa is one of a growing number of freelance workers.

### Hani Shawwa
#### Freelance Broadcast Journalist

**A-levels:** Economics, History, German
**AS-level:** Maths
**Degree:** BA African Studies, German Studies, University of Birmingham
**Postgraduate Diploma:** Broadcast Journalism, University of Central England in Birmingham

In Hani Shawwa's view, radio is an excellent medium in which to work.

He explains, 'It's relatively easy to send out stories on the radio, which means you can have a really quick response to news stories. Broadcasting on television is a more complicated and time-consuming business, which means radio often gets in first with breaking news. I also like the fact that radio allows you to be creative and to paint your own picture of a situation.'

While at university Hani became involved in student radio, producing a weekly comedy news slot with a friend. After graduation he took a temporary administrative job in London, but soon became bored, began thinking seriously about his future, and applied for a place on the broadcast journalism course at the University of Central England in Birmingham.

The course lasted nine months. In Hani's words, 'There was a strong practical element, learning how to operate equipment and undertaking practical assignments and work placements. I spent a month's work placement with BBC Radio West Midlands, which was a steep learning curve, and where I learnt how to write decent copy and work with producers and editors.'

On completing the course Hani started to work freelance for several local radio stations including BBC Radio West Midlands and BBC Radio Shropshire, Herefordshire and Worcestershire, and for the Radio 4 programmes *Today* and *You and Yours*.

He had a three-month contract with a local radio station in Staffordshire and freelance work at BBC Pebble Mill, followed by a contract with BBC Radio Stoke. At present Hani is doing production shifts for the new BBC Asian Network and working as a reporter for *You and Yours*.

Looking back, he says, 'The first year after finishing my course was really tough, but work is coming in now and I'm certainly finding my way around the West Midlands!'

# Fact

### *Not all job vacancies in the media industry are advertised*

It's often a case of being in the right place at the right time. This makes networking and building up contacts vital.

Unfortunately there are a lot of very talented people who don't make it in the media because they don't have the type of personality needed to get on. It isn't just a question of making phone calls, but ringing back at least five or six times, making sure people remember who you are.

## Fact

### *It's better to take any job than to hold out for the right one*

Graduates with impressive degrees must be prepared to take very lowly jobs and to make themselves useful washing up and sweeping floors. Many of them do voluntary work without payment in order to try and get a foot in the door.

However poorly paid a job is and however trivial the work, it is far better to be in work making contacts and impressing people with your energy and talent than it is to be at home making phone calls in pursuit of the perfect opening.

## Fact

### *Work experience is important*

It's vital. Whatever career you opt for, finding out exactly what it involves is essential. Work placements during degree courses and in the holidays provide something that no amount of time spent in a library can equal – a taste of reality.

Ideally, work placements should last at least a month and preferably longer, to give you time to prove yourself, make strong contacts and impress people who are in a position to offer you further experience or even a job. When you read the profiles in this book you will see that over and over again work placements lead to real work.

Whatever career you follow, the importance of work experience should never be under-rated. In Chapter 3, Leanne

Bracey, Picture Editor, *Harpers & Queen* gives advice on how to gain the most from a work placement.

## Fact

### *I need to do a lot of research before deciding on the best way forward*

You do, and there is plenty of help available.

Skillset is the national training organisation for broadcasting, film and interactive media. Its website (see Chapter 15) is full of advice and information on careers and training.

There is a skillsformedia resource centre, skillsformedia advice line on 08080 300 900, and a Skillset/British Film Institute database of undergraduate, postgraduate, full-time, part-time and short courses.

Rhian Griffiths is now established in a career in television production, but this is after a long struggle, seizing every opportunity, however small.

### Rhian Griffiths
**Television Production Co-ordinator**

**Scottish Highers:** English, History, Biology, Art, Music, Modern Studies
**HNC:** Media Production and Analysis, Telford College, Edinburgh
**Degree:** BA Media Production, Bournemouth University

'The first time I applied for a place at Bournemouth I was rejected, so I took a year-long HNC media course at Telford College in Edinburgh.

'I was initially interested in camera and lighting, as photography was a big interest of mine. At Telford I gained an interest in the moving image and learnt about lighting techniques as well as radio broadcasting. The college had good television studios and editing facilities and during the course I decided to take a degree in media production and applied again to Bournemouth.

'In my second year I saw an article in *Broadcast* magazine explaining that BBC Scotland had commissioned a new drama entitled *Hamish MacBeth*. Zenith Productions was having its pre-production period in Edinburgh, my home town. I wrote asking if the company would take me on a work placement.

'The employed runner wasn't familiar with Edinburgh, so I was sent off on errands around the city, while she concentrated on other arrangements. When filming started on location near the Isle of Skye, I stayed with a friend's family for two weeks and watched the filming process.

'As well as the usual jobs – photocopying, making tea – I was given the task of breaking down some of the scripts ready for scheduling. I realised that there was a lot more to drama than directing and camera work and began to consider it as a future career.

'Just as I handed in my dissertation in my final year I got a call from the production manager of *Hamish MacBeth* saying she was looking for a runner for a new project, a Carlton drama series, *Thief Takers*, about the flying squad. I moved up to London that weekend.

'When the production was about to finish the production manager recommended me to a producer friend and for the next nine months I was runner on *Soldier Soldier* (series VI) for Carlton Television. From there I got another running job on a big budget British feature film, *Swept from the Sea*, shot in Cornwall.

'Moving back to television I was offered promotion to producer's assistant on the next series of *Soldier Soldier*, on the understanding that we would shoot a period drama called *Heat of the Sun* straight afterwards. This was very exciting as I was being given a lot of responsibility for the first time.

'Originally my job on *Heat of the Sun* was based in England, but I went out to Zimbabwe to help the producer for a few weeks. It was a fantastic experience but exhausting, and when I returned home I took two months off – my first break for two and a half years.

'My next job was as post-production secretary on *Maisie Raine*, a television detective series starring Pauline Quirke. My responsibilities included making sure we had the appropriate licensing rights for music, ensuring everyone involved knew the final dubbing dates, and grading dates for each episode.

'A lot of paperwork is involved when you hand the programme over to the broadcaster. You have to make sure that all correct rights are obtained and various forms are completed in order that transmission goes smoothly.

'There is a billing form listing the actors and their character names, plus the director, producer and writer and a short synopsis of the programme. This information ends up in television listing magazines. Other forms list music cues and time codes to show technical reviewers where the music comes in and there is a fuller synopsis should the programme ever be repeated.

'When a further series of *Maisie Raine* was commissioned I stayed on pre-production, working with the producer while he developed storylines and found writers for the second series. I then carried on into the filming of this series right through to post-production.

'Afterwards I worked as production secretary on a BBC in-house drama about a lawyer, called *Fish*. It was there I met a highly respected line producer who offered me my next job, which was a step up to production co-ordinator for a new Channel 4 drama, *North Square*, a series about young lawyers, shot in Leeds. This was a job approaching management status with a lot of responsibility.

'In a drama series co-ordinators oversee the whole production, dealing with up to six different episodes at a time, while prepping another two episodes and dealing with two more in different stages of post-production. It's a highly organised job and you need your eyes and ears open all the time.

'My jobs include booking equipment and making sure it appears at the right place, ordering action vehicles, making sure there's enough film stock, booking hotels, distributing scripts and dealing with amendments, informing everyone of film schedules, making sure they know what they are filming each day. Usually I have a runner and production secretary working under me and I have to make sure they know which tasks to do.

'Every day I have to produce a progress report on the previous day's filming, including how long it took to complete filming, additional costs involved, how much film stock was used and the current running time of the script.

'I usually arrive at work about 6.30am to do the progress report, because there can be a lot of interruptions once filming starts.

'After *North Square* I worked as a co-ordinator on two series of *Dalziel and Pascoe* in Birmingham and *Two Thousand Acres of Sky* in Scotland. At the moment I'm taking a couple of months off while I buy a flat and settle in. Then I start work as co-ordinator on a new television pilot series.

'You need total commitment to do my job, working 12-hour days, usually without a chance to eat your lunch in peace. When filming you sometimes work one weekend in two, which can be tough. The work is really challenging and no two days are ever the same. I love the variety and wouldn't want to work in any other area. I'm just so glad I saw that article in *Broadcast* magazine – it was a stepping stone to my future.'

# 2 Choosing the right course

Media degree courses vary enormously, from the highly academic to the extremely practical.

Depending on the course you choose you could spend the majority of your time in a library and in lectures, or you could be working in a recording studio learning for yourself exactly how to use the latest equipment.

Studying for a degree in any subject is not cheap. The majority of graduates finish university with debts of around £10,000. In order to make this investment worthwhile, you need to do your own research into courses and make sure that the one you choose is right for you.

With hindsight, Andrea West, who is doing her best to get that first break in the media, feels she could have made better choices.

### Andrea West
**Temporary Clerical Worker with the Environment Agency**

**A-levels:** Media, English Language, History
**Degree:** BA Media Arts, Royal Holloway, University of London

'At present I'm doing administrative work for the Environment Agency because I need to support myself. In my spare time I chase up all the opportunities I can find in radio work.

'I'm quite prepared to work on a voluntary basis in the evening and at weekends, just to get my foot in the door, but it's not easy. I live in Lincolnshire and I'm making contact with independent and BBC radio stations in my area and with hospital radios. I also go through all the newspapers looking for openings.

'When I started my degree studies there was the possibility of a work placement as part of the course, but unfortunately it didn't happen. I really regret this because a work placement looks good on a CV. It proves you have some idea of what a job is really like and, just as important, it's a brilliant opportunity to make some good contacts.

'Looking back I feel I should have chosen a more practical degree course and once at university I should have chosen my options more carefully, bearing in mind that I was wanting a job in the media industry in radio or television.

'Still, there's no point in dwelling on the past. In around six months I hope to be in a position to move nearer to London where there are more opportunities in the media. My priority now is to find myself that break and I'm determined to do it.'

## Take a look at yourself

Is your main aim a media-related career? If so, do you want to operate high-tech equipment in a television or video studio? Do you want to design interactive games and programmes? Do you want to appear on screen as a broadcaster or presenter, or would you prefer to work on a newspaper or magazine?

Do you have an academic approach to media studies? Perhaps you want to look at why so many people read tabloid newspapers and examine the social impact of television on society. Are you looking for a career in the media, or is media studies an academic choice in the way other people are choosing history or geography?

## Joint degrees

Many universities offer joint degree courses, which means you can study two subjects rather than one. Options include media studies with a foreign language, business studies, accountancy, chemistry, conservation, hospitality, leisure or sports studies. The list is almost endless and for students who have a broad range of interests, or who are undecided about a future career, joint degree courses can be a good choice.

## Foundation degrees and Higher National Diplomas

Foundation degrees and Higher National Diplomas are a good option for those who want to take a highly practical course. A number of people profiled in this book opted for one of these routes, or an industry-approved professional qualification, rather than a degree because they wanted the most hands-on training possible.

## Don't judge a course by its title

Some course titles, such as Broadcast Media, Media Writing, Advertising, Marketing and Communications, might seem to describe a course's content clearly, but courses with similar titles vary enormously from one university to another.

As a general rule courses such as Media Production and Media Technology tend to have a more practical slant than those entitled Media Studies, or Media and Culture. Courses such as Lens Media, Video Production and Media Electronics are likely to be specialised and to appeal to people who have a clear view of their career direction. However, it doesn't pay to take anything for granted.

To make matters even more complicated, media-related courses may not even have the word 'media' in the title.

Communications courses should be of interest to students looking at media-related courses. These usually cover all aspects of human communication including linguistics or the study of language; semiotics, which is the study of signs and symbols; anthropology and psychology. Some Communications courses also include a practical approach to making messages including videos, film, sound and graphic communication.

When looking at different courses, don't stop at the first year. This is often spent looking at the broad strands of a subject and at this stage many courses can look remarkably similar. It is in the second and third years, when there is an element of choice, that differences can be clearly seen. The more practical courses offer options such as audiovisual systems, sound and moving image production and digital processing techniques. Theoretical course options are more likely to cover the effects of censorship, and the development of the mass media.

The majority of courses are a combination of theory and practice and include lectures, seminars, practical workshops, essays and project work. On most courses students are required to undertake a piece of original work in their final year. This could take the form of a written dissertation, but on some practical courses it could be a practical project such as video or audio production, graphics or computer animation.

## Ask the right questions

Make visiting college open days a priority and when you're there make a point of talking to students on the courses that interest you, as well as to lecturers.

Facilities on a media course are important. Check that dark rooms, studio space and equipment, editing facilities and camera equipment are up-to-date and well maintained. Equally important, find out how much access you would have to these facilities. Would you be free to use them as you wished?

If you are drawn to a particular course because a member of the staff has a high reputation and you want to study under this person, make sure he or she will be actively involved in running the course when you are there. A person's name may be listed on a staff list, even if he or she is about to take a sabbatical, or work in Australia for the next 12 months.

# Work placements

If your ambition is to work in the media, you need to check that your college has strong contacts with the industry and offers work placements to students. These usually take place during holidays and provide an unbeatable opportunity not only to experience what the work is like, but also to impress people and make contacts.

Try to find out which organisations offer placements to students and how long these placements are likely to be. Remember the general rule is, the longer the placement, the better.

Kate Morton is in her final year of a Media Arts with Video Production degree course at Thames Valley University in London. Having researched her options before applying, she finds the course does offer what she wants.

### Kate Morton
**Final-year Student, Media Arts with Video Studies, Thames Valley University, London**

**A-levels:** Theatre Studies, Media Studies, German, Sociology

'When choosing a course I looked for one that included video, television and film work in a college in or close to London.

'I've really enjoyed the course at Thames Valley because it combines both theory and practical work. The media arts section means attending lectures and seminars covering subjects such as the effect the media has had on society. Video production involves using equipment, making films, screen writing.

'At the beginning of the course, we learnt the basics of using the equipment. This can be daunting at first and while you don't need to be very technically minded, you do need to feel confident handling equipment and be able to pick things up quite quickly.

'I was lucky when it came to editing because I had some experience of using Apple Macs, which in some ways are different from PCs. The equipment at Thames Valley is really great and there's not usually any problem booking it out.

'Everyone has to write a dissertation or produce a practical project in the final year. I've been lucky enough to have my plan for a ten-minute film accepted and at the moment I'm putting a lot of thought into it.

'During the summer I've worked with a communications company specialising in website design where I learnt a lot. My ultimate ambition is to work in film or television, on pop promos. Competition is really intense and I'm already writing letters, building up contacts and trying to find work on a voluntary basis, which is often the way in.'

# 3 Work placements

The people in the profiles in this book make it clear how important work placements are. Over and over again they relate how a placement led either directly to the offer of a job, or to making important contacts with someone who at a later date proved to be helpful.

Many media-related courses include work placements, but there is no reason why you shouldn't find your own. Don't wait until you've started a course to look for a placement. Try to find one before you apply, so you have a good idea of what work in the industry entails.

As a starting point, ask teachers or college staff for help, or go along to your local Connexions office. Look in the Yellow Pages telephone directory for companies in your area. The Skillset website (see Chapter 15) is also full of useful information and contacts.

Once you have a placement, take it just as seriously as you would a paid job and gain as much from the experience as you can.

Tom Weller is someone who discovered for himself the importance of work placements.

**Tom Weller**
**Video Co-ordinator, ITV London News**

**A-levels:** Business, Communications, Theatre Studies
**HND:** Professional Broadcasting, Ravensbourne College, London

'The course was highly practical. The lectures were hands-on with two large studios and the latest broadcasting equipment. We covered a great deal of technical and engineering theory, which at the time I didn't think I would use directly, but it's certainly paying off now.

'We spent time on work placements during the course. I worked on *The Bill* and *Friday Night with Jonathan Ross* and *Lennie Henry In Pieces, This Is Your Life, Tomorrow's World* and *Jack Dee's Happy Hour*. These placements are vital because very few job offers depend on formal interviews. If people like you and there's an opening, you're offered it, usually before it's advertised externally.

'My first job was as a runner, a general assistant doing anything that needs to be done – putting scripts together, dubbing tapes, dealing with the post and answering phone calls from viewers.

'Six months later I'm learning editing on the job and hope to train as a vision mixer in the near future. The work demands total commitment, coming in on days off to do some training and working various shifts that either start at 5am, or end at 11pm. If sociable hours are a priority, a broadcasting career isn't for you. But I love it and it certainly beats working for a living!

'Making the right impression and setting up contacts are the ways into work. You have to market yourself, which is easier said than done when you're feeling low because you've worked hard at college and still haven't got a job in the industry.

'A lot of people in my year at college are still looking for work. The secret is getting a foot in the door, grabbing the first opportunity, whatever it is, and working your way up from there.'

Knowing how important placements are can make them daunting. What do companies want from a student? How can you impress people in such a short space of time?

Leanne Bracey, Picture Editor with the magazine *Harpers & Queen*, took a media-related degree. As a student she went on work placements, which helped to establish her career. Today her job includes looking after students on work placements. This is her advice on how to get the most from your time with a company or organisation.

## Preparation

Do your homework in advance. Find out all you can about the organisation offering you a placement and the products or services it provides.

Prepare yourself as far as possible for the work you will be doing. For example, if you are going to work in an art department, try and learn how to scan and find out something about digital imagery.

Familiarise yourself with the layout of the neighbourhood, so when you're sent out on jobs you can be trusted to do something quickly and efficiently without getting lost.

## First impressions

Be yourself. Smile, be friendly and confident, but not gushing or arrogant.

Remember you will be working in a busy environment and people may not have a lot of time to spend with you. Don't take this personally, but remember time is precious and staff won't have time for long chats.

Make the most of the time people give you. Ask questions, listen, be interested and try not to look blank!

## Punctuality

Try never to be late. If there is a problem always phone and let people know.

## Trust

No matter how much you know, be prepared to do what might seem simple routine tasks, because these are what you'll be given, especially at the beginning. People have to learn to trust you before they give you more complicated and responsible work. Do whatever you are asked to do as well as you can. Keep your work area tidy because it makes a good impression if you have a tidy workspace.

Write points down in a notebook for reference. Don't use scraps of paper because this makes you look scatterbrained!

If after a couple of weeks you are still being given 'rubbish' jobs, take a look at yourself and try to work out why you are not being given more interesting work. Look at ways you can improve how you tackle the work you are being given.

## Communication

Ask if you're not sure. People do want you to get things right because if you don't they'll have to do it again.

If you have a problem share it with the person who is responsible for your placement. However, you might have to choose your moment. When someone is clearly very busy, it isn't the time to discuss your placement.

## Useful tips

★ Learn to love organising
★ Start making lists
★ Develop a good memory
★ Always have a back-up plan and a good filing system
★ Try your best to get on well with everyone
★ Don't lose your sense of humour
★ Try to have a mentor, someone whose opinion you respect, and don't be afraid to ask him or her for advice

## What can I do with... a media studies degree?

★ Be prepared for knock backs
★ Know your industry, find out what is happening in other companies.

A work placement certainly gave Leanne the break she needed.

### Leanne Bracey
**Picture Editor, *Harpers & Queen***

**A-levels:** English Literature, Design Communications, Art
**Degree:** BA Journalism, Surrey Institute of Art and Design

'When I began my degree course I had my sights set on a career in journalism, but then I found my interests lay in a different direction.

'My course had a strong creative element. Students in my year started up a college magazine called *Velvet,* which is still going strong. When I became involved in the layout of the magazine I realised that my interest was in pictures rather than words.

'During my course I had a work placement at *Cosmopolitan* and took the opportunity to talk to the designers about how they had got into work. They told me a job was coming up as an art assistant at *Harpers & Queen* and that I should apply.

'I thought about it but decided as I was still at college it was too early to apply for that type of job. To my surprise, just as I was finishing my degree course, I had a phone call from *Harpers & Queen* asking if I'd like to apply. On my way home after the second interview, I was coming to terms with the fact that I hadn't got the job, when my phone rang and I was offered it.

'As art assistant I did just about everything that was needed to maintain and organise the department: running around, scanning in pictures, researching illustrations and helping to organise shoots.

'The picture editor worked part-time, which meant that at times I was left to cope on my own. The situation was daunting, but looking back it worked in my favour. A full-time picture editor was appointed and I worked under her for about a year. When she left I was asked to apply for the job.

'I organise all the images for the magazine except for the fashion shots. I commission freelance photographers to do work. I contact established photographers and negotiate with them to use their existing work. Otherwise I use picture libraries to find the right images for a feature.

'People sometimes think that because *Harpers & Queen* is a glossy magazine, we have a bottomless pot of money for illustrations and can pay a fortune. The truth is we work to a strict budget and I have to negotiate fees very carefully.

'My job is demanding. Deadlines have to be met and problems are always cropping up. I do find I take my worries home with me because that's the nature of my work, but I love it.'

# 4 Job titles and what they mean

It is not possible to cover all the job opportunities in the media industry in the following pages, because there are simply too many. A further complication is the fact that similar jobs have different names in different sectors.

What follows is a look at some key jobs in the industry plus the type of training needed and the skills and qualities required to do the work. The jobs are divided into three sections: administrative, creative and technical, and are listed in alphabetical order.

There is a growing trend towards flexibility in the media industry, which means that a person may have more than one area of responsibility and may have a combination of job roles.

## Administrative jobs

**Producer** – has overall responsibility for managing the project, bringing together finance, cast and crew, making sure budgets are kept and completion dates met.

*Qualities and training.* Some producers are very involved in the creative side of a project, choosing scriptwriters and actors, while others are more concerned with the business aspects and have a finance or law background.

Nobody comes into the industry at this level. The career route is usually as a runner and then assistant director posts. A wide knowledge of the industry is vital and so are patience, tact and stamina.

**Production Assistant** – works as producer's personal assistant, co-ordinating all aspects of production. A lot of the work is administrative: typing and distributing memos, putting in script changes, hiring equipment and booking rehearsal space. Some production assistants work on continuity, making sure details remain the same from shot to shot.

In radio work where production teams are often very small, production assistants may also operate equipment and do live interviews.

*Qualities and training.* Good organisational skills, patience, tact and enormous energy are needed. These are the people who arrive early and stay late.

**Researcher** – gathers information and contributes ideas, finds people prepared to appear on a show, books celebrity guests and looks up background information on them, preparing a list of questions for an interviewer. A researcher working on current affairs programmes can carry out in-depth investigations of controversial issues.

Radio researchers are often called broadcast assistants and are involved not only in research but also in writing and making programmes.

*Qualities and training.* While a degree can be an asset, the important qualities are good communication skills, the ability to make people feel at ease and a constant source of good ideas.

**Runner/General Assistant** – does anything: fastening microphones, moving equipment, making tea and coffee, buying sandwiches and newspapers. Some runners work for the entire production, while on large projects such as feature films there could be a floor runner, art department runner and production runner.

*Qualities and training.* For most people, this is the starting point where newcomers gain a real understanding of what is going on.

## Creative jobs

**Animator** – works in different areas including cel animation (the traditional drawn method), claymation (animating clay figures), or computer generated images. Some animators work in all of these areas.

*Qualities and training.* Most animators have studied the subject at college, although some companies do offer training. Creativity and a strong artistic talent are vital and so is patience as the work is painstaking.

**Costume Designer** – works closely with the director to provide suitable costumes and accessories while keeping to a set budget.

*Qualities and training.* Knowledge of period costume is necessary, as are strong organisation, design and sewing skills, and the ability to motivate other people. Most designers start as costume assistants.

**Director** – has overall creative control and makes most of the creative decisions, working closely with photography, production and costume departments and directing the actors and designers, camera and sound crews.

*Qualities and training.* Nobody, whatever their background, enters the industry at this level. Directors start as third or fourth assistant directors (see below). They need to be good communicators and decision makers, able to stay calm under pressure, with a great deal of artistic imagination.

**Editor** – interprets the requirements of the director, sometimes by physically cutting the film, but more usually by using sophisticated computer technology. Some editors are largely creative and others more technical.

*Qualities and training.* Strong creative, visual and technical knowledge, good communication skills and the ability to get on with people.

**Floor Manager/Assistant Director** – works closely with the director, making sure everything is where it should be. The number of assistant directors varies according to the size of the budget. The first assistant director is the most senior and has most contact with the director.

The more senior assistant directors are in charge of the studio during recording. They book rehearsal space, co-ordinate rehearsals, pass on instructions to sound and camera crews, organise positioning of props, and are often in charge of health and safety matters, making sure sets are safe and exits are not blocked. Junior assistant directors look after the actors, making sure they are dressed and made-up on time.

*Qualities and training.* Some but not all directors have media studies degrees. Patience and good humour are needed, plus strong organisational skills.

**Graphic Designer** – designs title sequences and credits and graphic effects within programmes. In the interactive media, designers create exciting visuals including online and Internet projects.

*Qualities and training.* A graphic design degree or similar qualification is usually necessary, as are good computer skills and knowledge of different graphics packages plus artistic talent and a constant supply of good ideas.

**Hair and Make-up Artist** – works with the director and costume designer to create the styles and appearance required for different productions. Some specialise in special effects such as moulding, scarring or wounds.

*Qualities and training*. A relevant qualification such as an NVQ is essential. Specialist short and long courses are available. As well as artistic talent, tact and good communication skills are vital.

**Props Manager** – sources props such as furniture, china, guns, art objects – whatever is required for the production – and makes sure they are in the right place and kept safely.

*Qualities and training*. Props managers have usually been to art school and have a good visual eye and knowledge of period furniture and objects.

**Scriptwriter** – either thinks of an original idea or is commissioned to provide a script from an existing idea.

*Qualities and training*. A lot of scriptwriting courses are available, but many scriptwriters have no formal training. Writing talent is vital, but so is self-motivation and determination as this is a particularly difficult area to enter.

## Technical jobs

**Engineer** – works in a number of areas including design, transmission, installation and service.

*Qualities and training*. A relevant qualification such as an NVQ, City & Guilds, HND or a degree is required. There is a shortage of qualified engineers in the media industry.

### Vision

**Camera Operator** – records action on film. Feature films, television dramas and many commercials are shot on film, while documentaries, live television programmes and corporate videos are shot on videotape. Recent years have seen the introduction of digital film and cameras.

Television studio productions usually use between three and six mounted cameras, which are moved around the floor. Portable cameras are also used and sometimes cameras mounted on cranes to take pictures from above. During recording, pictures from different cameras are fed into a bank of monitors for the vision mixer to select the most appropriate.

On outside broadcasts covering important occasions such as sporting events, or royal weddings or funerals, there is a large team of camera operators with cameras fitted on tripods or mounts and a mobile control room. Usually outside news teams are very small: often just a presenter, sound recordist and camera operator.

*Qualities and training.* Most camera operators have worked as clapper loaders (see below) and focus pullers. Good technical ability and a wide knowledge of cameras and lenses are essential.

**Clapper Loader** – loads and unloads the film in the camera magazine, marks the shots with a clapper board, writes the lab reports and prepares the rushes or unedited film for the labs at the end of each day.

*Qualities and training.* This is a very responsible job as a mistake can cost a day's filming. Reliability, technical knowledge and tidiness are important skills.

**Director of Photography** – works closely with the director to put his or her ideas into practice. Some operate cameras themselves while others leave that to the camera operator.

*Qualities and training.* This is a senior role gained after years of camera experience. Today many directors of photography have taken specialist cinematography courses. A high level of technical knowledge is vital, plus good communication, creative and decision-making skills.

**Focus Puller** – follows focus on moving subjects in front of the camera, taking detailed measurements and changing focus settings when needed.

*Qualities and training.* Focus pullers usually begin work as clapper loaders. Technical knowledge is important and so is a good eye for detail.

**Grip** – handles the many different types of equipment that enable the camera to move.

*Qualities and training.* Technical knowledge, good communication skills, flexibility and good physical co-ordination are required.

## Sound

**Boom Operator** – holds the long boom or metal arm to which the microphone is attached, as close to the action as possible.

*Qualities and training.* Most sound technicians start as assistants and work their way up. They need good technical ability, perfect hearing and a good level of attention.

**Sound Editor** – builds up layers of sound, using a mixture of live sound, sound footage and sounds created by sound effects.

*Qualities and training.* See Boom Operator.

**Sound Effects** – known as Foley Artists in the trade, they add extra sounds and special effects such as creaking floorboards, owls hooting and slaps and groans in fight sequences. This is done with a mix of high-tech and low-tech methods.

*Qualities and training.* See Boom Operator.

**Sound Recordist** – records sound on location or in the studio. The sound is monitored through headphones and the recordist usually synchronises his or her work with the camera crew.

*Qualities and training.* See Boom Operator.

**Special Effects** – manages explosions, car crashes, rain and snow, often enhancing material using computer technology at the post-production stage.

*Qualities and training.* Art and design and engineering qualifications are good starting points, so is a job as a junior assistant. Awareness of health and safety issues plus a calm, sensible approach are important as is imagination and the ability to think around a situation to achieve the right effect.

# Training

There is no set training path to be followed in order to work in the industry. However, there is a definite trend for freelance work and FT2, the national training provider (see Chapter 15), offers training opportunities for people seeking a freelance career in the following areas:

★ Art department assistant
★ Assistant editor
★ Camera assistant/clapper loader
★ Grip
★ Make-up hair assistant
★ Production assistant
★ Props assistant
★ Sound assistant
★ Wardrobe assistant
★ Researcher.

Training operates like an apprenticeship and leads to a Skillset professional qualification. Those taking part need a high level of commitment. They must be certain they want a career in their chosen area and have had relevant work experience. Eighty per cent of the time is spent training with practitioners. Days are long and trainees have to relocate to London. There are no fees to pay and trainees receive a monthly training allowance of around £720.

Selection is tough with around 70 applicants for every place. About 90 per cent of applicants have studied some form of media-related programme. However, talent, commitment and practical knowledge of the industry are definitely the major requirements.

FT2 does not train scriptwriters, directors or producers. Information on training in these areas is available from Skillset, the sector skills council for the audiovisual industries (see Chapter 15).

Skillset together with the British Film Industry (BFI) produces a comprehensive guide to media courses, which includes useful information, descriptions of courses and contact details. For further information contact the national media careers helpline: 08080 300900; www.skillsformedia.com.

# Broadcasting and the audiovisual industries 5

The broadcasting industry covers television and radio, while the audiovisual industry includes film, video and the interactive media.

This chapter contains sections on television, radio, film and video. In each section it looks at job opportunities and major employers, and profiles young people working in that sector of the industry.

Many people move from one industry to another, using their skills wherever they are required. Multi-skilling is now common with one person doing several jobs, for example a camera operator may also work on lighting and sound and undertake some editing work.

Whatever the medium, productions are usually divided into three sections:

★ pre-production – scripting and planning
★ production – filming and recording
★ post-production – recording special sound and visual effects, mixing or dubbing voice, music and special effects soundtracks together.

## Television

The television industry may be dominated by a few household names like the BBC and Granada, but there are many medium-sized production companies and small operators in the frame.

Digital technology has been developing fast since the early 1990s and future developments are likely to include:

★ more choice
★ greater convenience
★ increased contact between viewers and broadcasters
★ communication between televisions and PCs
★ electronic programme guides allowing viewers to organise
their own schedules
★ immersive television with wide screens making viewers feel
part of the programme (likely to be developed for the pay-
per-view market for big sporting events).

Many programmes already have an interactive element where
viewers have their own input via a website, voting for a
particular person, or chatting to show business personalities.

## Interactive television

Interactive television owes its existence to the merging of
computer and telecommunications technology with traditional
television. Today websites and computer games can be
accessed via a television and soon films and television
programmes will be accessible via a PC.

At present most interactive television focuses on banking or
shopping services, but the future is wide open. For example
viewers could receive information on participants during a
sporting event or take part in a quiz show while watching it on
the screen.

Programme schedules could be a thing of the past with
viewers able to watch whatever they want when they wish. It
is already possible to pause an actual programme thanks to the
development of TiVo systems.

## Employers

**Broadcast television companies** – national and regional
BBC TV and ITV network companies, which have their own
studios and equipment. Some staff are permanently employed,

36

but many are taken on for a fixed term when needed. Companies also buy in programmes from abroad and commission around 25 per cent of programmes from independent production companies.

**Satellite and cable television companies** – most job opportunities are in creating link and promotional material for programmes and films which are largely bought in.

**Independent production companies** – there are over 1,000 in the UK, making TV programmes, films and commercials, pop promos and videos. Some have their own studio facilities and employ production staff, but the majority have only a few permanent staff, bringing in freelances and hiring studios and equipment when required.

### Employment opportunities

Interactive television is bringing with it lots of new opportunities for technicians and programme makers from traditional media backgrounds, as more programme commissioners look for an interactive element in programmes, television companies merge with Internet providers, and film makers use computer and digital technology.

As a systems operator with GMTV, Barry takes recording material from all over the world and transfers it into different formats.

#### Barry Hinchey
**Systems Operator, GMTV**

**BTEC National Diploma:** Media Studies, Kingston College
**HND:** Professional Broadcasting, Ravensbourne College, London

'When I left school I joined my Dad working in mechanical services, fitting heating and ventilation systems, but it wasn't for me so I did a GNVQ and then a BTEC National Diploma in Media Studies.

'After the GNVQ course I thought about trying to get a job as a runner and working my way up, but decided against it and went on to take the BTEC. I'm dyslexic and it was not until I went to college that I learnt to spell with confidence, started to enjoy learning and began to see the point of education.

'I wanted to build on this and I did well on the BTEC course, gaining distinctions and top of the year awards. I chose Ravensbourne because the college is well recognised in the industry and the course is so practical. The course lasted for two years and most of the days were long with work from 9am to 6pm, with a compulsory work placement during the summer holiday – if you don't do it you fail the course.

'My placement was at the BBC working with the cutting editor on BBC News 24. I was asked to go back after the course, but I found cutting on a live programme was really frightening. At that stage I didn't have enough confidence to do the job and so I turned down the offer, took a three-week break, began applying for other work and was accepted by GMTV.

'My college course was very hands-on and involved a lot of time working with equipment. This gave me a good start at GMTV because from the very beginning I knew what I was doing.

'My ambition is to work as a programme director. It's a creative job, deciding which shots go up on screen.'

Although Liz was certain she wanted a career in television, she decided to take an academic degree and went to Sheffield to read French.

**Liz Thorne**
**Gallery Production Assistant, attheraces**

**A-levels:** Theatre Studies, History, French, General Studies
**Degree:** BA Professional Broadcasting, Ravensbourne College, London

'I knew during my first term studying French that I'd made a mistake. The social life was good, but the course was not for me. After a year I left and went back to a temporary job as a chef.

'My Dad is a broadcasting engineer and went to Ravensbourne 30 years ago. Courses there are highly specialised and intensive. I decided to apply for a place on the professional broadcasting accelerated degree course.

'It lasted for two years with a compulsory work placement through the summer. The first part was basic training in all areas of television work. Then we moved on to more theoretical work and a dissertation. I did mine on television shopping channels.

'Because of my Dad's job, I knew quite a lot about broadcasting and the studios and equipment didn't bother me at all, but the work placement was a nightmare. I worked as a runner on a location shoot in London from 7am to midnight and was responsible for checking sound, cameras, production, cleaning, health and safety, preparing food and looking after guests.

'After a short time I was exhausted and looking back I should have told the college what was happening, but I stuck it out, which did give me a fair amount of satisfaction.

'During my final year I visited the International Broadcasting Convention in Amsterdam where I bumped into two people who had worked with my father years ago. Sometime afterwards I took a phone call for my father and mentioned that I was looking for work. I sent in my CV and was invited for an interview.

'When I got there the two people on the other side of the table were the pair I'd met in Amsterdam. They offered me a job as a floor assistant with attheraces (pronounced 'at the races'). I took it and went straight back to college to tie up all the loose ends and sign off.

'The company provides 18 hours of live racing coverage a day, from UK racecourses and US courses in the evening. My day

**What can I do with... a media studies degree?**

began at 6am. I checked the studio, making sure it was tidy and safe, with no equipment blocking the exits. I washed up from the previous day, briefed the presenters, welcomed guests, put on their microphones, organised coffee, tea and lunches and distributed newspapers. Between programmes I re-positioned the remote control cameras, which are operated from the gallery.

'After a few months I was promoted to gallery production assistant. This involves checking and correcting scripts, producing a breakdown of the show and working out exactly how long each part of the show is to last. I'm one of those people you see on TV shows running around with enormous stopwatches.

'You do have to be pushy to get on in this world, which means a lot of talented people don't make it. You also have to be prepared to start at the very bottom, no matter how good your qualifications might be.'

Unlike Liz, Duncan Bain opted for a first degree in an academic subject and found it worked very well.

## Duncan Bain
### Studio Operator, Enteraction TV

**A-levels:** History of Art, Architecture, Religious Studies
**Degrees:** BA History of Art and Philosophy, University College London
BA Professional Broadcasting, Ravensbourne College, London

'My school was quite academic and knowing how fickle the media industry can be, it seemed like a good idea to have a second string to my bow. I enjoyed my course but I never lost sight of my ambition to work in the media.

'After graduation I worked for the BBC on a six-month contract as a senior librarian in the Resources Department. Every day we collected the broadcast tapes from the previous night, catalogued them and ticked them off on a spreadsheet. The work wasn't connected with broadcasting, but it was a great experience working for the BBC.

'I then took the two-year degree course in Professional Broadcasting. It was made up of both practice and theory, compared with the HND course, which was almost completely practical.

'Throughout the course I was working freelance to help fund my studies. I was a freelance videotape operator on GMTV and was a camera assistant at the MOBO award ceremony.

'Once the course finished I was lucky enough to get a two-month contract as a DVD quality control technician. All that time I was surfing the net for work and luckily got the job with Enteraction, which makes programmes for corporate television channels.

'A major client is a travel company and we produce programmes featuring holiday destinations and hotels, a type of on-screen holiday brochure.

'I've been at Enteraction for 18 months and I'm responsible for setting up the studio and recording the show. This includes the use of a holocloth or reflective curtain, which provides a perfect blue background on to which computer-generated images can be superimposed. Part of my job involves using an Avid Express editing system. I'd used the system occasionally at college, but now I'm using it all the time.'

# Radio

At one time, families would sit together in the living room, listening to the radio. Today the nature of listening may have changed, but around 89 per cent of adults listen to the radio for at least three hours a day. The majority of motorists tune into the radio to help pass the time behind the wheel, and listeners often develop a great loyalty for a particular station.

The growth of radio looks set to continue with new digital licences. As the cost of these falls an increasing number of people are expected to buy them in order to enjoy near-CD quality sound, a vast range of channel choices and the ability to display text and picture images.

Commercial or independent radio has recently become less highly regulated by the Radio Authority, which awards licences. It used to require commercial stations to keep to a strict programming structure, but now the situation is more relaxed.

A growing trend is the development of bi-media covering television and radio at the same time.

## Employers

**Network radio** – BBC Radios 1, 2, 3 and 4, plus regional and independent channels have their own studio facilities and staff and make many of their own news, drama and documentary programmes.

**Local radio stations** – there are over 150 of these in the UK, broadcasting across set geographical areas or to ethnic communities. They employ technicians who are multi-skilled and able to operate a range of equipment. Presenters prepare news and programmes and do an element of operating themselves.

**Independent audio production companies** – make taped readings of novels, training tapes and recordings of conferences. This type of work is often closely linked to the music and recording industry.

**Facilities houses and suppliers** – these include video editing suites, sound mixing studios, camera, sound and lighting equipment companies, which source locations and create computer graphic sequences. All offer services that can be hired as and when they are needed. Some employ staff to operate the equipment while others have a list of freelances to be used as required.

At sixth form college studying for her A-levels, Natalie took up the option to study for two City & Guilds qualifications in the evening. At that point she already knew she wanted a career in the media.

## Natalie Barrass
### Radio Presenter, BBC 7

**A-levels:** Media Studies, French, Theatre Studies, English Literature
**City & Guilds:** Radio and Press Journalism, Video Production
**Degree:** BA Professional Broadcasting, Ravensbourne College, London

'I had a Saturday job in a sandwich bar and my boss's father had been a presenter on the TV programme *Tomorrow's World*. My boss told me Ravensbourne College ran good courses so I applied.

'I found my own work placement at college as a runner and receptionist with Digitas, an online marketing company. Within the first few months of being at college I had replied to an advertisement in *The Stage* magazine to audition for a promotional video for a well-known fruit-flavoured alcoholic drink. The drink was awful and we weren't paid for our four days' work, but I kept in touch with a couple of people from the company who now ask me to do regular freelance work.

'After graduation I panicked about having no work. It was a miserable time and I ended up moving back home to my parents in Southampton and taking a temporary job issuing disabled parking badges.

'I got so frustrated with this that I took the opportunity of cheap flights to America and booked myself a month's trip to Los Angeles on the advice of a good friend – thinking that maybe I could make some contacts over there. I had my show reel converted to NTSC and set off in January.

'I didn't get any work, but I did meet some pretty crazy people and returned to the UK with renewed enthusiasm and drive. Before I left I had gone to a careers fair and was contacted with the offer of work experience at Portsmouth

Television, to take place after my return from America, booking in guests, researching topics and briefing presenters.

'A friend then told me that a temporary runner was needed for the BBC hospital drama, *Holby City*. The work only lasted for a few days but it was a foot in the door. While I was there I heard about work going with BBC Children's Television. I applied and was successful.

'Over a third of my pay went on travel between London and Southampton. Once a week when I had a late finish followed by an early start, I slept top to toe in a single bed with a friend in her tiny room so I could get up at 4.30am and be at work on time.

'My second day on the job found me dressed up as an Easter Bunny prancing around the studio with Pete the Pie, who left soon afterwards to take up a radio job. When he e-mailed over opportunities for radio work, I applied and got an audition. This took the form of a mock live programme and it was a nightmare. I had to work with three children I'd never met before. I had less than 30 minutes to prepare and when I was supposed to read out e-mails from viewers, I couldn't find them in the pile of papers I'd dropped on the floor.

'Not surprisingly I wasn't offered a job straight away, but I was told they liked my style and would keep in touch, which they did, with an offer of work as a presenter on a children's programme, *The Big Toe Radio Show* on the new digital radio station BBC 7.

'The show is aimed at pre-teens and is accessed via computer and television as well as digital radio. It's live between 4 pm and 6 pm and includes interviews, competitions, stories and news.'

# Film

Around ten years ago the British film industry enjoyed an up-turn with the success of films such as *Four Weddings and a Funeral*, *East is East*, *The Full Monty*, *Shakespeare in Love* and

*Brassed Off.* This period of success peaked around four years ago, since when there has been something of a downturn.

Watching films is a major activity among 18- to 30 year-olds and technological developments such as videos and DVDs have brought film viewing into most homes.

The move towards making some films digitally has cut costs dramatically and there are exciting opportunities for people with the right skills and determination in the film industry. However, most people work freelance and invest their own time and money in training. At present the workforce tends to be unbalanced with too many qualified people trying to work in areas such as directing and too few available to work in areas such as engineering.

## Employers

**Feature film production companies** – the name may conjure up images of huge operations, but the majority of British companies are nothing like this. A company can often be no bigger than a producer and a secretary who employ freelance staff to work on individual productions.

Since graduating Claire Bee and her business partner Todd Kleparski have each had two jobs. Claire has been managing the trade counter of Film Stock Centre Blanx, which sells motion picture film stock and consumables, and Todd has been running at Rushes, a post-production house. This is while also running their own film production company.

## Claire Bee
### Film Producer

**A-levels:** English Literature and English Language
**Advanced GNVQ:** Media Communication and Production
**Degree:** BA Professional Broadcasting, Ravensbourne College,
London

Kleparski and Bee Productions specialises in the production of
short films, commissioned by individuals or companies and often
used as calling cards or shown at film festivals. As emergent film
makers, Claire and Todd are able to hire studios and equipment
at a lower cost than professionals.

Recently they have given up their day jobs to produce their first
full-length feature film. Money to shoot the film has been raised
by private investment and by taking advantage of the Enterprise
Investment Scheme. Finance for the post-production budget is
currently being sought.

The director of the film approached Claire and Todd after he
gained some private investment in the project. As producer Claire
is involved in every aspect, from attracting finance to putting the
film into the hands of sales agents who negotiate its sale.

Claire graduated a year ago and looking back sees her time at
university as 'valuable growing-up time'. However, she is
sceptical about media courses.

'My course was very practical and well regarded in the
industry, but looking back, I would have learnt almost as
much leaving school as soon as I could and getting a job as a
runner. Too many people with media degrees are protected
from the real world. They leave college only to realise that,
despite their qualifications, they have to take jobs as runners
in their chosen field.

'I think colleges should be much more up-front and honest
about the problem of obtaining work within the broadcast
and media industry than they usually are. I also feel strongly
that media courses are often far too broad. The subject is
enormous and trying to cover everything means nothing is

done properly, which is why media degrees can get such a bad press.'

Despite working in an industry where who you know often matters more than what you know, Claire has no family connections in the film world, but she is still determined to make it.

'I was lucky enough to interview Sir Alan Parker, who heads the National Film Council and directed films such as *Bugsy Malone, Angel, Evita, Fame, The Commitments* and *Angela's Ashes*. I asked him if people like me were ever going to get a foot in the door. He said "Talent always gets through eventually, you just have to believe in that", and I do.'

## Video

Today video means CD-ROMs and DVDs as well as tapes. These have a huge capacity and offer a great many interactive facilities. DVDs can store up to four hours of broadcast quality pictures with multiple audio and video tracks, which means one DVD can store different versions of a video in numerous languages. As broadband develops, video will be distributed over the Internet, making it even more flexible.

Videos are used for training, company communications, public relations, sales and marketing, as well as for recording live events such as concerts and weddings.

### Employers

**In-house film/video/audio-visual units** – some big organisations have units that make promotional or training videos for their own use. Some employ full-time video technicians although many use freelance staff.

**Corporate video makers** – the corporate video market is bigger than the entire UK film industry. The reason for its popularity is that it is simple, cheap to use and a very effective way of getting a point across.

As a freelance video technician, James is self-employed.

## James Hudspeth
### Freelance Video Technician

**BTEC:** Media Technology
**HND:** Technical Operations, Ravensbourne College, London

'I took the two-year full-time HND course in technical operations at Ravensbourne and while I was there spent part of my summer holiday working on *The Big Breakfast*. This led to paid work on the show and to a place on the freelance rota, which meant I could be called to work as a technical floor assistant at any time.

'My job involved setting up monitors and video feeds and any special equipment for a programme such as that required for games. Working on *The Big Breakfast* while still at college meant a long day and plenty of early starts, but it was well worth it for the experience.

'Since leaving college I've worked on a number of freelance video systems and set up several installations for private broadcasting companies: rigging up systems, video videotape machines and monitors.

'In a few weeks I begin full-time work as a video engineer, recording and transmitting programmes for a studio and transmission house in London's East End. I'm really where I want to be with this job. When I was at college I thought I wanted to be an editor, putting programmes together, but as time went on my interests became more technical.

'I'm doing what I want to do, which makes me incredibly lucky because lots of people I know in this industry haven't got jobs.'

# Journalism  6

It is the role of the journalist to keep people informed of what is going on, whether on a global, national, regional or local level. Journalism divides into:

★ broadcast journalism – television and radio
★ print journalism – newspapers and magazines
★ online journalism – a relative newcomer growing in importance and bridging the gap between print and broadcast journalism.

## Broadcast journalism

### The job

Covers work for national and local radio and television. At first sight, reading the news might not seem difficult – just a case of sitting there and reading out what you're told. In fact newsreaders and reporters are all trained journalists, usually with years of experience of gathering and writing up news. Most newsreaders not only read the news but write much of their own material. They organise and carry out interviews, both live and recorded, working closely with a radio or television crew, and are involved in decisions about presenting a story.

The job of newsreader does not really exist at local radio level where the news is read by reporters or newsreaders who are actively involved in news gathering.

Journalists also work as correspondents either reporting on issues such as education, politics or health, or on news from particular areas of the world, such as the Middle East.

**What can I do with... a media studies degree?**

Not all broadcast journalists appear on screen or broadcast on the radio. Off-screen journalists work largely on computers, recording interviews, attending press briefings and chasing up stories.

Starting salaries in broadcast journalism vary between BBC and commercial radio and television. An average starting salary is around £13,000.

## Qualities needed

★ Excellent communication skills – the ability to express yourself clearly
★ A clear, pleasant microphone voice
★ Natural inquisitiveness
★ Tenacity and determination to search for the truth
★ Tact and diplomacy to deal with people who are distressed, nervous or unwilling to be interviewed
★ The ability to stay calm under pressure and to remain objective
★ Self-confidence
★ Flexibility – news stories can change seconds before broadcast or even on air if a big story breaks
★ Sound technical skills
★ The ability to work as part of a team
★ Knowledge of rules of grammar and punctuation
★ Enthusiasm and willingness to work unsociable hours.

## Getting in

The majority of the skills required for a career in journalism are gained on a media degree course. However, graduates with a degree in any subject can make a career in journalism. As in all media-related jobs, success lies in having the right skills rather than possessing particular academic qualifications.

Whatever route you take you will need evidence of your skills and enthusiasm in the form of articles published in student newspapers, freelance articles in local free or paid newspapers, or involvement in community or campus radio stations.

Many journalists go into broadcast journalism after working in print journalism (see the 'Getting in' section of Print journalism). To go straight into broadcast journalism usually requires a first degree in any subject followed by a postgraduate broadcast journalism course. Some television and radio companies run direct-entry training schemes for graduates, but competition for a place on these is fierce. Courses are usually advertised in the national press.

The Broadcast Journalism Training Council produces a list of recognised postgraduate courses (see Chapter 15). Some courses concentrate on the specific skills of radio or television or online journalism; others have bi-media programmes covering radio and television; others cover all three sets of skills.

There has been a growth in the number of cable and satellite television channels and independent radio stations, and the imminent arrival of digital audio broadcasting (DAB) should also create more job opportunities. Opportunities for online journalism are also growing.

Broadcast journalists usually start as reporters in local BBC and independent radio newsrooms.

### What can I do with... a media studies degree?

As head of news on a local radio station, Mike James heads a team of five and has editorial control, or the final say on what news is broadcast.

**Mike James**
**Head of News, Minster FM**

**A-levels:** Theatre Studies, Art, History
**Degree:** BA Art History, University College London
**Diploma:** Broadcast Journalism, London College of Printing

'I joined Minster FM, a local radio station based in York, eight months ago as a journalist, reading hourly news bulletins and taking part in the longer 6 o' clock news programme, as well as compiling news items and travelling around Yorkshire reporting on events.

'After completing the diploma course at the London College of Printing, I was offered two jobs, one in Wolverhampton and one in York, and I really enjoy working as a broadcast journalist.

'When I went to university I had no idea what I wanted to do for a career and chose to study art history purely because the subject interested me. While at college I did some voluntary radio work and when I saw the course advertised at the London College of Printing, decided to apply.

'The course was very practical and a complete change from my degree course. Apart from media law and shorthand classes, we spent very little time in the classroom. We did a lot of script writing, practised interview techniques and studio operations. The course lasted eight months and after the first two we were responsible for running the college's news centre two days a week and were out and about all over London.'

Charmaine Cozier took the same postgraduate diploma course as Mike, but arrived there by a very different route, after a career as an accountant.

## Charmaine Cozier
### Editor and Journalist, Star 106.6 Radio News

**A-levels:** English, History, Religious Studies
**Degree:** BA Librarianship and Information Studies, Polytechnic of North London
**Postgraduate Diploma:** Broadcast Journalism, London College of Printing

'I worked for ten years in the corporate finance division of an accountancy firm and qualified as a certified accountant, but a job in radio was always my dream. I worked as a volunteer on a hospital radio and even did a week-long course to try and get it out of my system, but it was still there.

'When thinking about a career change, the difference in salary level was a key consideration. I sat down and worked out my finances and realised I could survive. I had a cheap mortgage and a car. I knew I could always fall back on temping in the finance sector to earn more money if I didn't get a job. The time had come to do something about my dream, or forget it.

'I rang up BBC and commercial radio newsrooms for advice and was told that as I knew exactly what I wanted to do, I should go for a specialised broadcast journalism course rather than a more general media qualification.

'The diploma course was brilliant and grounded in the real world. We had regular visits from editors and journalists from major stations who gave us a lot of valuable advice. There were official work placements towards the end of the course, which resulted in a lot of students, including myself, being offered jobs.

'When I started the course my plan was to go into financial news, but I discovered I really liked dealing with general news.

'Star 106.6 covers the Windsor, Slough and Maidenhead areas, which is a great news patch, plus we get a good response to stories from listeners. I've never regretted going into radio. I love it.'

# Print journalism

## *The job*

The two major sectors of print journalism are:

★ newspaper journalism
★ magazine journalism.

Both types of work have similarities: following up leads, building up contacts, carrying out interviews, working to strict deadlines. Newspapers are usually more concerned with following up news stories as they happen, while magazines take a long-term look at issues. Both national newspapers and magazines use feature writers for longer articles and for specialist subjects such as motoring, travel or health.

Journalists work as:

★ **Editors** – in overall charge of the publication, hiring staff, working closely with advertising departments and printers. On local papers they are involved in writing and design. National newspapers and magazines have a number of editors in charge of particular areas of work such as news or features.
★ **Sub-editors** – designing pages, cutting and adjusting copy and selecting photographs.
★ **Production editors** – linking the editorial department, designers and printers.
★ **Art and picture editors** – in charge of the overall appearance of the publication.
★ **Commissioning editors** – liaising with freelance journalists, photographers and designers, organising work and negotiating rates of pay.

Salaries for trainee journalists vary from publication to publication, but are usually in the region of £9,000–£14,000. Freelance rates vary enormously.

## Qualities needed

Qualities needed for a career in print journalism are basically the same as those for broadcast journalism, but without the need for a clear voice.

## Getting in

More than 130 daily and Sunday newspapers are published in the UK, plus 800 weeklies, 1,000 local free newspapers, 2,000 consumer magazines and 4,500 business and professional publications. The total number of magazines on the shelves has grown by over 30 per cent in the last ten years. Even so, there is a lot of competition for jobs and most vacancies attract dozens of applicants. Approximately 30 per cent of journalists are self-employed and working freelance.

Non-graduates and graduates with degrees in any subject can make a career in journalism. Success lies more in having the right skills than in possessing particular academic qualifications. Many of the qualities sought by editors, such as enthusiasm, flexibility, strong communication skills and the ability to get on well with people, are those gained from a media degree.

Some trainees are recruited straight from school or university, usually on to local papers, after taking tests in writing ability and current affairs and are offered an on-the-job training contract usually lasting two years.

The majority enter by the pre-entry route after graduation or in some cases after A-levels. This means taking a course approved by the National Council for the Training of

Journalists. These are usually one year full time, although some colleges offer fast-track courses for graduates lasting 18–20 weeks. Part-time courses are also available. Further information is available from the NCTJ (see Chapter 15).

Training for magazine journalists is either by direct entry on to a training scheme run by a periodical or magazine, or by taking a periodical journalism course accredited by the Periodicals Training Council (see Chapter 15).

Helen Gabriel is currently taking a nine-month postgraduate diploma in newspaper journalism at Cardiff University and is hoping to find a job on a regional daily paper.

### Helen Gabriel
**Postgraduate Student, Cardiff University, School of Journalism**

**A-levels:** English, History, French, Photography, General Studies
**Degree:** BA Media with English, Falmouth College of Art

'My undergraduate course was largely theoretical, looking at the development of communications and examining the role of the media. Some people feel that media courses should not be academic, but I don't agree.

'I wanted an academic degree course and what I learnt is very useful on my journalism course. It's important for journalists to realise the impact their writing has on the reader and my media studies help me to do this. For me media and English was a good combination of subjects.

'In contrast my journalism course is very practical. Much of the time is spent in a simulated newsroom developing and improving practical skills such as writing and shorthand and learning how to use QuarkXpress, the Apple Mac design programme.

'While I was at Falmouth I had a work placement on the *Daily Mirror* where I learnt a great deal. I made some very positive contacts and was given real jobs researching and writing articles for the finance section, which helped me to master the tabloid style of writing. Without the placement I don't think I would have been offered a place at Cardiff because you have to prove that you're serious about a career in journalism.

'Coming up is a placement on the *Manchester Metro*, which should also be a great experience.'

Samantha Chapman went straight into work as a trainee journalist after graduating with a first degree.

## Samantha Chapman
### Print Journalist, Aldershot Newsgroup

**A-levels:** English Literature and Language, Sociology, Spanish, General Studies
**Degree:** BA Journalism, Surrey Institute of Art and Design

'I knew I wanted to be a journalist by the time I had taken GCSEs. I opted to take English language at A-level because it gave me an opportunity for creative writing and then went on to study for a specialist journalism degree at Surrey Institute of Art and Design.

'My degree course was very practical and "hands-on". We had work experience placements in the first and the third year and I spent some time on the art desk of the *Daily Star*. Throughout the course we were encouraged to go out and find our own stories.

'In the final year we not only had to write a 10,000-word dissertation but also a 3,000-word feature. I wrote my feature on *Big Brother*-type television programmes, looking at their audience appeal, the people who watch them and those who take part in them. The work involved carrying out a number of interviews.

'While at college I studied both broadcast and print journalism. I enjoyed the broadcast part of the course, but I always felt certain that print journalism was for me and that I wanted to work on a newspaper.

**57**

'I went straight into my job after graduation. I'm based in Aldershot and work on a bi-weekly newspaper, which means we have two deadlines a week – Monday and Wednesday. My work involves going out and about in the community, attending court sessions and local events. I also enjoy the layout part of the work, designing newspaper pages.

'As I work I'm undergoing training, improving my shorthand and keeping a log book of cuttings of the articles I write.'

Toby Williams is a press photographer.

### Toby Williams
**Photographer, *Blackpool Gazette***

**Scottish Highers:** Maths, Biology, English, Art
**Degree:** Marine Biology, University of Stirling
**Press Photography course:** Norton College, Sheffield

'After graduating with a marine biology degree I did some travelling, worked as a chef and in a scuba diving shop.

'As the years passed I began to feel I needed a proper job. My father was a keen photographer and I'd taken photographs of my travels, so when I saw a job advertised for a press photographer with the *Edinburgh Evening News* I applied.

'The editor saw my holiday snaps and offered me a fortnight's work experience so I could see what the job involved. I loved it and applied for the press photography course at Norton College Sheffield.

'Press photography is very different from other types of photography and Norton College is the only place in the country that runs courses approved by the National Council for the Training of Journalists (NCTJ), so it's highly regarded in the newspaper world.

'I had two courses to choose from: press photography and photojournalism. The difference between the two is that the photojournalism course covers the use of extended captions to accompany photographs. I opted for press photography.

'In order to do the course I had to take out a bank loan to keep myself and to buy a car and a camera. To support my studies I did weekend voluntary work on the *Sheffield Star*, so there was no time for a part-time job.

'The good thing was that the course is geared to teaching students the skills they need to get pictures and find work. On the first day of the course in September we were told the college would be disappointed if we were still there at the end of the nine-month course.

'By January I had a job with the *Blackpool Gazette* and I was the second to leave. The *Gazette* is a daily paper with two weekly papers in the same group. The job is really interesting and no two days are ever the same.'

# 7    Public relations

Public relations (PR) is concerned with reputations. PR professionals are the guardians of an organisation's reputation. Their aim is to establish good relationships and sound lines of communication between the organisation and the groups or target audiences that are important to it.

For example, a multinational manufacturing organisation could well have a number of target audiences with which it needs to keep in contact, including national governments, shareholders, pressure groups and employees.

Communication is about listening as well as talking and PR is not simply about giving out information but also about setting up contact between different groups, carrying out research, evaluating the findings and feeding back information to the management of the organisation, so they can be considered when making future decisions.

## The job

It is not only commercial organisations that use PR professionals. National and local governments, political parties, universities and charities are just some of the organisations that call on their services.

Large organisations and some world-famous personalities have their own in-house PR staff, working exclusively for them. Others use a PR consultancy, which works for a number of clients.

The first stage in a successful PR campaign is to discuss with the clients what they require, then to gather information, analyse it and from these findings draw up a strategy and put it into practice. An important part of the work is measuring the success of a campaign afterwards, as clients need to know their money has been well spent.

Starting salaries in PR vary a great deal. A PR officer working in-house for an organisation and an account executive in a PR consultancy are likely to earn in the region of £20,000.

## Qualities needed

★ Excellent communication skills, both written and spoken
★ A pleasant, relaxed manner and the ability to get on well with people even in difficult situations
★ Quick thinking, flexible approach to problems
★ The ability to work well as part of a team
★ Strong organisational skills
★ The ability to cope with pressure
★ A lively interest in current affairs.

Many of these skills are gained from a media studies degree.

## Getting in

Around 48,000 people work in PR jobs in the UK. Just over half, approximately 56 per cent, work in-house for different companies and organisations, while the rest work for PR consultancies. Some PR specialists work freelance.

A media-related degree is helpful, although graduates with a degree in any subject can go into PR. For those who are certain before they go to university that a career in PR is for them, it is possible to take a specialist first degree in the subject.

Entry into PR is highly competitive and a job can attract hundreds of applicants, which is why some people opt to do a postgraduate course in order to make themselves more marketable. A list of courses approved by the Institute of Public Relations (IPR) can be found on the IPR website (see Chapter 15).

Work experience is vital as it is the only sure way to make certain a career in PR is right for you. It is also a sign to potential employers that your interest is serious and you have done as much as you can to make yourself as marketable as possible.

PR vacancies are advertised in the local and regional press and in the following publications: *PR Week, Press Gazette, Profile* and in the *Guardian* media supplement.

Once in a job, PR personnel often work towards a professional PR qualification. These are offered by the Communication, Advertising and Marketing Education Foundation (CAM), the Chartered Institute of Marketing (CIM) and by the Institute of Public Relations (IPR). A list of approved qualifications can be found on the IPR website (see Chapter 15).

As the head of the corporate team in a PR agency, there are two distinct strands to Nichola's job.

### Nichola Sharpe
**Account Director, Freud Communications**

**A-levels:** Communication Studies, English Language, English Literature
**AS-levels:** History, Sociology
**Degree:** BA Media and Communication Studies, Loughborough University

'Central to my role is protecting the brands of my clients, either by creating positive media coverage or by diluting potentially negative coverage in the media.

'My clients are big companies and part of my job is making sure that positive news such as winning awards for product design, or opening a new manufacturing unit, is reported in the media.

'The other side of my work is crisis management. This means advising clients on how to handle any bad news that might emerge. The crisis could be serious, for example rumours about a company's financial situation, which might result in a loss of confidence among shareholders, or criticism about the standard of a product, which could mean a loss of customer confidence. In such cases I and my board director would be in 24-hour contact with the client, giving advice on how to answer questions and writing statements to be issued to the press.

'Freud Communications is a privately owned independent agency employing around 100 people. I head a team made up of another account director, two account managers, two senior account executives, a team assistant and a research manager.

'My interest in public relations started early and I did voluntary PR work for my sixth form college. While at university I had a work experience placement with a PR company in Colchester, near home.

'After graduation I became an account trainee with a large agency. I was in charge of the photocopier and did a lot of running around, which is the best way to start.

'From there I moved to a top PR agency and then to a small specialist agency, each time for a job offering more responsibility. My present job, which I've been doing for several months, is my biggest challenge yet.

'During my time in PR I've built up my contacts with the national press and with trade publications. I've recently organised two big media events for one of my clients, with photo opportunities and interviews.

'Organisation is the key to my work. I have to be conscientious and I have to be a 'plate spinner', able to cope with several issues at once. I also have to be well ahead with my work. It's no good leaving something until the last minute because a crisis could arise that demands all my attention.

'In some areas of PR there is a "who you know" mentality. The school you went to and the number of strings you can pull can be important. This is annoying because it means jobs don't always go to the best people.

'Having said that, I do thoroughly enjoy working in PR and it's certainly where I want to stay.'

Henry Lawes works as an account executive supporting account managers and directors in a marketing, public relations and communications agency. While at college he was not considering a career in PR but has found that the skills he gained have equipped him well for the work.

### Henry Lawes
**Account Executive, Beatwax Communications**

**A-levels:** Geography, History, Theatre Studies, General Studies
**HND:** Professional Broadcasting, Ravensbourne College, London

'As an account executive I have a close relationship with the photocopier, supporting senior members of the account team.

'I also design and build websites for clients, which involves using the technical skills I learnt at college. Looking back, the most important thing I gained from my course was multi-skilling. This includes undertaking several tasks at the same time, working competently on different pieces of equipment, plus core skills such as communicating successfully with people, finding out information and, most important, how to network and develop contacts.

'The reason I've gained these skills is my course was completely practical. I considered taking a degree course, but opted for the HND because of its content. Before going to Ravensbourne I started another course at a different college. This was about 70 per cent theory and 30 per cent practical, and after a few weeks I'd learnt enough to know I'd made a bad decision.

'As part of the HND course I spent 11 weeks on a placement with Yorkshire Television. The length of a placement is important because if it's only a couple of weeks, it's not long enough to make an impression or be given any real responsibility. I was lucky in being given real work to do and I ended up being given a credit on screen for my research.'

# 8 Publishing

(See also Chapter 6, on careers in journalism.)

The publishing industry covers:

★ newspapers and magazines – the largest group being business-to-business publications, which rarely if ever appear on the newsstand. Another growth area is in-house magazines produced by organisations for their employees. There is also a huge range of specialist magazines, for example for the owners of particular types of car, dog breeders, family historians and caravan enthusiasts.
★ books and journals – the majority of the thousands of books published every year are not for the mass market, but are specialist publications such as educational textbooks and scientific, technical and medical books.
★ directories and databases – more than 2,500 companies in the UK publish consumer and business information, funded either by sales of copies or by advertising.

There are also online jobs available in all these sectors.

## The job

Work in publishing falls into four categories:

★ editorial
★ design
★ production
★ sales and marketing.

**Editorial** – covers researching, writing, editing and commissioning material.

Commissioning editors research the market to find out what people want to read, then decide on new titles. They find authors to write the work, brief them on what is required, deal with any difficulties that arise, check and amend completed copy and decide on the layout and final appearance of the publication.

Publishing companies receive unsolicited work from authors who send it in the hope that it will be accepted. Commissioning editors organise readers to deal with the vast pile of unsolicited material they receive, passing back to them the work that merits a closer look.

**Design** – includes setting out the material so it looks attractive and is easily readable. This work is largely computerised, so knowledge of computer design programmes such as QuarkXpress is necessary.

**Production** – involves the overall organisation of the publication, making sure copy is complete, liaising with printers and keeping to schedule.

**Sales and marketing** – covers informing interested parties about the publication and persuading them to place orders and to advertise in its pages.

Starting salaries vary, but an average figure is around £15,000.

## Qualities needed

To work in publishing you need:

★ Good organisational skills
★ Strong communication skills, both written and spoken
★ Strong technical writing skills, with a high level of accuracy in spelling and punctuation, for editorial work
★ An up-to-date knowledge of literary trends – what type of books are being read

★ An outgoing, persuasive personality for work in sales
★ A good business eye
★ The ability to work with and motivate other people
★ Confidence to put forward your ideas
★ Well-developed computer skills.

These are all skills to be found among media graduates.

## Getting in

Publishing is very competitive and getting in requires more than a degree. In most cases relevant work experience is vital. Employers are looking for practical knowledge of publishing, either through work experience, holiday jobs, or involvement in college or university publications. Often a specialist postgraduate course is also needed.

First degree courses in publishing and courses with publishing options are available at many universities. Postgraduate diplomas and degrees are also offered by a number of universities and colleges; the Publishing Training Centre has a list of these (see Chapter 15). A great deal of useful information, including training and job opportunities, is to be found on the Publishing National Training Organisation website (see Chapter 15).

The way into a career in publishing is often through a job as an editorial assistant with a publishing company. Editorial assistants do whatever is required: photocopying, researching possible new areas of interest for publications, making contact with authors, drawing up agreements and proofreading material. This way they gain the experience they need to apply for a more senior post, such as commissioning editor.

Short training courses, some by distance learning, in subjects such as proofreading, on-screen editing and print buying are run by the Publishing Training Centre. Some larger publishing companies run their own training schemes.

For some jobs a knowledge of proofreading could be helpful. This demands an eye for detail and knowledge of the correction symbols used in the process. These can be self-taught with the aid of a book such as the *Writers' and Artists' Yearbook*, or studied through a correspondence course.

To find a job research is essential, visiting book fairs, making contacts with people in publishing and finding out about openings, often with small specialist publishers.

Before going for an interview, find out all you can about the company. If the post is with a specialist publication, do some homework on the subject.

Publishing jobs are advertised in the national press, but smaller companies often advertise in specialist publications such as *Press Gazette*, *Media Week*, *The Bookseller* and *Publishing News*.

Lisa Rutter went into her publishing job after completing her first degree.

### Lisa Rutter
**Deputy Head of Editorial, Business Hotline Publications**

**A-levels:** Spanish, English, Law
**Degree:** BSc Media and Communications, Loughborough University

'Business Hotline Publications provides business advice material for around 200 clients wanting to make contact with small businesses. For example, a company might commission an article on an aspect of self-employment from Business Hotline Publications to put on its website, in order to attract the attention of people running small businesses.

'My job includes finding freelance writers to research and write the articles, commissioning the work, dealing with contracts and overseeing the progress of the work, making sure everything is running smoothly and keeping to schedule.

What can I do with... a media studies degree?

'At Loughborough the media studies course included a number of different options, such as psychology and sociology, which I found very interesting. While at university I began to think about a career in publishing, but had no direct work experience, and after graduation panic set in.

'I applied for all sorts of jobs, but kept coming back to the idea of publishing. I had an interview for a job with the Eclipse Group, which specialises in business publications. I didn't get the job, but the company recommended me to Business Hotline Publications where there was a vacancy. For the first few months I worked on the sales side and then I moved across to editorial.'

Catherine Cronin studied English literature for a first degree and went on to take a Master's degree in publishing.

### Catherine Cronin
#### Contracts Manager, Random House Children's Books

**International Baccalaureate**
**Degrees:** BA English Literature, University of Aberdeen
MA Publishing Studies, City University, London

'My job is to handle the contracts for children's books. The contracts fall into two types. Head contracts are signed between the authors and illustrators working on a book and the publishers, and they cover matters such as schedules and payments as well as the length of licence and the rights and territories granted. I sometimes deal directly with the authors or illustrators, but often negotiate with their agents.

'The second type are subsidiary rights contracts or third-party licences covering issues such as merchandising arrangements – for example games or clothes featuring characters from books, and translation and film rights.

'Selling subsidiary rights and negotiating subsidiary contracts is crucial in the case of children's books, because third-party licences are important in helping to cover the cost of the book. In the case of picture books, a book may not be published if there are not enough translation deals.

**70**

'During my undergraduate course, I realised that I wanted a job working in the real world where I could use my qualifications and my love of books. In contrast to my first degree, which was purely academic, my publishing course had a strong practical bias.

'The course was firmly based in job reality and we were required to carry out fact-finding exercises and write reports. It also included a six-week work placement with a small independent publishing business, which gave me a chance to experience the reality of work and to apply what I had learnt at college.'

# 9    Marketing

No matter how well made a product is or how competitive its price may be, it will not sell unless it is what people want to buy. Before a new product is launched manufacturers need to be certain that it will sell not only in the UK, but in other areas of the world as well.

It is the job of marketing specialists to carry out research into current trends, to find out what people are buying, how much they are spending, how they like their goods to be packaged and presented. They develop new ideas for products, test sales opportunities and work with other departments in an organisation, to create products that meet customer needs or tastes and sell well.

In addition to researching and launching new products, marketing staff also maintain a brand's image, making sure the public are well aware of its existence.

The industry can be roughly divided into the following sectors, with the same principles used by marketing departments, whatever goods or services are involved:

★ fast-moving consumer goods – inexpensive, small products that customers buy regularly, such as sweets, drinks and washing powder
★ consumer durables – large expensive objects bought much less often, such as televisions and furniture
★ services – insurance, banking, holidays
★ business-to-business – covers products sold between businesses rather than to the public, for example manufacturing equipment and catering products
★ non-profit-making organisations – charities, hospitals, schools and universities.

# The job

Most large organisations have their own in-house marketing departments, which also incorporate public relations, advertising, design, research, development and sales.

Marketing can be divided into:

★ research – looking into what customers want from a product and how they feel about competitors' products
★ product development – working with design and production teams to make sure new products are what the customer wants
★ pricing – helping to work out a figure which that covers costs, gives a healthy profit and yet competes well with existing products
★ sales and distribution – calculating future sales figures so a company can meet future demand for products or services
★ promotion – working with staff in departments such as public relations and advertising to make sure a product enjoys a high profile with customers; this could include activities in stores, give-aways, competitions as well as advertising in the media
★ export – looking into existing competition and national tastes and cultural differences to see if a product is likely to sell in a particular country, finding agents to sell the product, organising export licences.

# Qualities needed

★ Strong communication skills, both written and spoken
★ A good business mind
★ Energy and enthusiasm
★ Problem-solving abilities
★ The ability to work with others as part of a team
★ Strong powers of organisation.

A career in marketing does not require a degree in a particular subject, but the qualities above are to a large extent those gained from a media-related degree.

# Getting in

An increasing number of graduates are choosing to take a full-time postgraduate course in marketing. Opportunities are available in many sectors, from food and drink manufacture to household goods such as washing machines and refrigerators, industrial machinery, insurance, travel and even schools and colleges.

Once in work, many employers encourage staff to study part-time for a Chartered Institute of Marketing or Institute of Export qualification.

There is strong competition for jobs in marketing and vacancies are advertised in professional publications such as *Marketing Week* and *Campaign*.

It was the nationally run Young Enterprise Scheme that made Linzi Chapman realise she wanted a career in marketing.

### Linzi Chapman
**Senior Account Manager, Black Cat Direct Marketing Agency**

**A-levels:** English Literature, French, Business Studies
**Degree:** BA Business Studies with Marketing, University of Greenwich

'When I was in the sixth form I took part in the Young Enterprise Scheme, which involves a group of people setting up a company and running it. My group set up a company making scented greetings cards and selling them. We sold the cards to our family and friends and gained bulk orders from a local department store and a craft shop.

'I was in charge of marketing the product and I loved contacting the media, communicating with people, promoting the cards. At the same time I also enjoyed the business aspects of working out our cash flow, calculating how many cards we could make and sell.

'By the time the project had finished I had decided on the sort of job I wanted and chose a four-year sandwich degree course with a year spent in work. My year in work was spent at Logistics International, a company supplying computer parts across the UK and Europe, and at Crammond Dickens Lerner, an advertising agency employing ten people.

'On the basis of my work placement I was offered a job with Crammond Dickens Lerner as a trainee doing bits of everything, which was a great way to gain experience of the work. Then the travel bug hit me and I went travelling to Australia where I worked for three months for the senior account director in an advertising agency in Sydney.

'Back home I found my present job with Black Cat. I have three clients, from different sectors: a finance operation, an outdoor media company and a reproductive healthcare charity. I run campaigns for them, holding regular meetings with clients, organising direct mail shots, press information, poster and television publicity and generally look after them on a daily basis.'

# 10 Advertising

The advertising industry is big business. Every year over £13 billion is spent persuading people to buy certain products, to support good causes, or vote for a political party. Government advertising campaigns also encourage people to live a healthy lifestyle, for example eating fruit every day, giving up cigarettes and taking exercise.

Advertisements appear in different types of media: newspapers and magazines, television and radio, on posters and on the Internet. They also come through the front door in the form of direct mail.

Although a great deal of money is spent on advertising, it is an industry that is quickly affected by economic change. When a company experiences financial problems, advertising budgets are often cut, so advertising is one of the first areas to be hit by a recession.

There are just over 1,000 advertising agencies in the UK with over half of them in London. The majority of these employ fewer than 50 people. Some agencies are very small and bring in freelance staff when necessary.

Advertising is a young person's industry and over 80 per cent of agency staff are under 40 years old. It can be an exciting world, well paid and lively, but it can also be precarious, with heavy pressure to meet deadlines and bring in new clients.

Starting salaries for graduates in advertising are around £17,500.

# The job

As in other areas of the media industry, flexibility is the order of the day, especially in small agencies. Individuals often have responsibility for a number of different areas and adapt their work to suit the needs of particular clients.

**Account Handlers** – include account executives and the more senior posts of account manager and account director. These are the people who have direct contact with clients and act as a link between client and agency.

When a potential new client approaches the agency, account handlers help to prepare a presentation or pitch for the new business. Once the agency has the work, they discuss with clients the products they want to advertise, the size of their budgets and what they expect to gain from the advertising campaign. They then brief the agency staff on what is needed and make sure clients are kept informed throughout the campaign. Most graduates come into advertising as account executives and those who are good at their job go on to become account directors.

**Account Planners** – make sure an advertising campaign is aimed at the right target audience. They decide the strategies that are needed, analysing existing research material and commissioning new research when necessary.

They need to know not only who buys the client's product, but who buys similar products, where, why and how often they buy them, and what their opinion is of the client's product and of the competition. Research continues throughout the campaign to measure its effectiveness.

**Media Executives** – decide where to place advertisements. They have to consider how much money is available and how this can be spent most effectively. To do this they look at the audience the client needs to attract, the newspapers they read, the television programmes they watch, places where they shop and eat and the routes they travel. Strong analytical skills are needed for this work.

A cool head is also a requirement because buying space can be a battle of nerves with a great deal of negotiation taking place, usually over the phone.

With the growth of new media opportunities such as cable, digital and satellite television, new radio stations and the Internet, the job of the media executive has become more complex, which has led to the development of placement agencies that specialise in placing advertisements.

**Copywriters** – together with art directors they form the creative team, which is responsible for designing the advertisements. The art director deals with the visual images and will usually have an art and design qualification. The copywriter writes the words to go with the images.

They are briefed by the accounts team and when creating the material they need to bear in mind not only the client's needs, but also competitors' advertisements. Art directors and copywriters need to form a strong team as they have to work closely together in a creative way.

Agency staff usually work on several accounts at the same time.

## Qualities needed

To work in advertising you need:

★ A lively, creative, flexible approach to work
★ Strong communication skills
★ Diplomacy and tact
★ An open manner, able to get on well with different types of people

★ Strong powers of organisation
★ The ability to work in a team
★ Self-motivation
★ Self-confidence to cope with difficulties
★ Energy, enthusiasm and determination
★ Good interpersonal skills.

The subject of a degree is less important than the skills of an individual, but the majority of the skills listed above are gained from a media-related degree.

## Getting in

The advertising industry is a very competitive one with many applicants for each job. While a degree is by no means an essential requirement, most jobs do go to graduates. The subject of the degree is less important than the qualities, skills and experience of the applicant.

A number of universities run degree courses in advertising and postgraduate diplomas and degrees, but these by no means guarantee a job.

There is no national training scheme for the advertising sector although the Communication, Advertising and Marketing Education Foundation runs certificate and diploma qualifications, and the Institute of Practitioners in Advertising runs training courses for advertising staff at all levels (see Chapter 15).

As with other areas of the media industry, getting into advertising takes determination and effort. Jobs are advertised in *Campaign, Marketing, Marketing Week* and *Media Week* and in the media section of the *Guardian*.

As an account executive in an advertising agency, Karina Rossi liaises between the client and the creative and artistic teams.

## What can I do with... a media studies degree?

### Karina Rossi
### Account Executive, Bray Leino

**A-levels:** English Literature, Art, French
**Degree:** BA Film and Media with Video Production,
Buckinghamshire Chilterns University College

'It is my job to talk over with the client exactly what is
wanted and then to brief the people who will be making this
reality.

'I also run the job bag system, which means I am responsible
for the administration of a job from the first briefing to the
final realisation. If a vital piece of paper is lost, it's up to me
to find it.

'Bray Leino is based in Devon and is one of the largest
advertising agencies outside London. There is a fair amount
of travel involved with my job as the agency needs to keep in
close contact with clients.

'It took me around six months to find a job after graduation,
during which time I decided against my original aim, which
was to go into television.

'My degree course was a combination of theory and practice.
Video production was very hands-on and practical, while the
rest of the course was largely theory. We looked at magazine
publication, analysing their content and readership, examined
different film genres and the development of radio and
television.

'I had television work placements on *Action Time* and on
*Celebrity Auction* and spent time with Peter Kerr Associates,
a company specialising in sourcing locations.

'My degree has given me that extra knowledge, both
theoretical and practical, which helps me in my job.'

# Retail and sales $\mathbf{11}$

## Retail

Retail is big business not only on the high street and in retail parks, but on phone lines and the Internet. A priority among the big retail stores is attracting bright, enthusiastic graduates capable of carrying the business forward.

### Qualities needed

Companies are looking for people who are:

★ Adaptable to changing situations
★ Able to work calmly under pressure
★ Enthusiastic and energetic about their work
★ Good organisers with strong leadership skills
★ Excellent communicators
★ Able to take responsibility yet work as part of a team.

Having a sense of humour helps too.

These are the type of skills gained from taking a media-related degree.

### The job

Most companies offer a chance to specialise in a particular area such as: retail management, buying, merchandising or public relations.

**Manager** – large stores have a general manager responsible for the entire store and business operation. Working with the general manager will be a number of other managers each with their own area of responsibility, for example customer service or a particular sales department.

**Retail Buyer** – buyers source and purchase goods for the store. Usually they are responsible for a particular category such as women's fashion or soft furnishings.

Most buyers go into the work through general management training programmes. The Chartered Institute of Purchasing & Supply offers training in various forms including distance learning, part-time courses and self-study, leading to professional qualifications (see Chapter 15).

Larger companies regularly use e-commerce methods to purchase goods so buyers need a high level of computer literacy.

**Retail Merchandiser** – plans, organises and monitors the distribution of goods to retail outlets.

The job involves a great deal of numerical calculations and for this reason recruitment interviews may include psychometric testing of numerical ability. Merchandisers work on computers and knowledge of spreadsheet packages and forecasting models is essential.

Working together with buyers, merchandisers decide the amount of stock to be purchased, forecast sales and profits, plan promotions and negotiate details of stock delivery. They visit production sites to check the manufacturing process, and when problems arise they need to act quickly.

Salaries for trainees are between £13,000 and £19,000. The manager of a large supermarket or a sizeable retail operation on a prime site can earn between £50,000 and £60,000.

### Getting in

Management trainee programmes combine on-the-job training with time in staff training centres. A graduate who completes a management trainee scheme can expect to be in a senior management position after three to five years. Some companies offer opportunities to work overseas.

Most companies have stands at careers fairs, websites containing careers information and booklets on training opportunities. Recruitment programmes usually run between October and May. Previous retail experience is welcomed, which means that part-time after-school and vacation jobs look good on a CV.

Sian Horner works in PR for the supermarket chain Asda.

## Sian Horner
**Administrator, Public Relations Office, Asda**

**A-levels:** English Language
**BTEC:** Media Studies
**Degree:** BA Media Studies with English, University of Sunderland

'I chose a joint degree because I wasn't sure whether I wanted to teach and so decided to keep my options open. One third of the course was English and the rest was media. This included cultural studies, two core practical modules and practical options such as public relations and print journalism.

'Before going to university I was a local correspondent on the *Northern Echo* and on my course I had a work placement at Sunderland Football Club press office.

'To help financially during my course, I worked on the night shift at the Asda supermarket and in my final year I wrote to the head office asking if there were any vacancies in the press office. The answer was no, but a few weeks before graduation, I got a phone call saying there was a job in the communications department.

'At my interview I was able to talk about my work placement and my newspaper column. It isn't enough to have a degree: you need evidence of serious interest in the work.

'When I was offered the job I was delighted. It wasn't public relations, but it was work with a good organisation and every job brings its own opportunities.

'After ten months there was a vacancy in the press office and I got the job. My work involves administration and public relations. Everyone in the office has a different area of responsibility for generating stories to the press. My area is customer service and it's up to me to make sure developments such as new and clearer signage or customer-friendly trolleys reach the press.

'I do some PA work for the Director of Corporate Affairs and some work on stores' public relations. Asda has over 250 stores and each one has a co-ordinator who covers public relations issues locally, contacting local newspapers and television with stories.

'We train the co-ordinators and if an event is going to be attended by the press, someone from the press office in Leeds will be there. So far my store visits have included trips to Cornwall, Southampton and Sheffield.'

# Sales

No matter how well designed and well priced a product is, it still needs to be moved on from the producer and sold. The sales team does this, by raising awareness of a product or service with potential customers and convincing them of its value.

Most sales activity is business-to-business, selling to shops, wholesalers and distributors who then sell to the retail customer or end user.

### Qualities needed

A career in sales is open to graduates with degrees in any subject, but a degree in media studies, together with subjects such as business, modern languages and journalism, is regarded very positively by many employers. This is because the skills and attitudes needed for a career in sales are strongly linked to those gained from studying a media-related degree. They include:

★ Strong communication skills, including a good telephone technique
★ Energy and determination to meet challenges and targets and flourish in a competitive environment
★ The ability to cope with disappointment
★ Good organisational skills
★ The ability to work as part of a team
★ Flexibility to adapt to changing circumstances.
★ An outgoing personality
★ A commercial business mind and product understanding
★ Being a self-starter.

## The job

Sales personnel usually work within a set geographical area. They are given sales targets to meet, usually on a monthly basis. There is an atmosphere of strong competition in most sales offices with pressure to exceed previous targets and achieve ever higher sales figures.

The work involves visiting customers, checking they have sufficient goods on display and in stock, introducing new products and encouraging them to place orders, dealing with queries and complaints and feeding back customer reaction to head office.

Sales opportunities exist in a wide range of products and services. Some companies, such as those selling pharmaceuticals, look for science graduates, but in other areas employers simply want graduates with the right qualities.

The majority of sales jobs involve a lot of time on the road and the work usually comes with a company car. Starting salaries range from around £14,000 to £23,000 and are often based on performance. In some cases payment is based partly or even completely on a commission basis, with sales personnel receiving a percentage of what they sell. Alternatively, significant bonuses are paid for exceeding targets.

Once in work, sales staff receive on-the-job training covering product knowledge and sales techniques. The Institute of Sales and Marketing Management and the Institute of Professional Sales (see Useful addresses) both offer a range of recognised qualifications.

## Getting in

Previous experience is not essential although work in any customer-related job is helpful.

Jobs are advertised in journals such as *Marketing Week* and *Marketing*, trade publications, and national newspapers such as the *Guardian*, the *Independent* and the *Daily Telegraph*.

# Travel and tourism 12

The world has become a smaller place. Around 50 years ago, a trip to France was considered adventurous, yet today holidays in the USA, Thailand and Australia are commonplace.

Not only do people travel further than they used to, they travel more often. Today many people take several trips abroad in the course of a year, at Christmas, Easter and during the summer, as well as taking regular weekend breaks.

Travel is not just a holiday or leisure activity. The majority of journeys are for business reasons and specialist business travel companies form an important part of the travel industry.

## The job

The leisure and business travel sectors have changed enormously in recent years. At one time work for travel companies was often seasonal and confined to the summer months. Today holidays are a year-round activity and many large companies offer good prospects for the right people.

Business travel has also seen big changes. At one time travel agents made their money by buying travel or accommodation for customers and receiving a percentage of the cost of the ticket as commission from the travel provider. However, airlines no longer pay commission, which on a long-haul flight could be quite significant, and instead pay a standard booking fee, regardless of the value of the ticket. This means that instead of travel agents being agents for a company and selling products for them, they are now managers, responsible for arranging the best possible travel for customers.

**What can I do with... a media studies degree?**

Business travel agents are not to be found in shopping centres and they are not household names like the major holiday travel companies, but they are considerable organisations.

A business travel agency or management company bids for work with organisations and if it is successful it takes over the organisation's travel arrangements for a set period of time, possibly one or two years. The agency's job is to ensure that members of the client organisation travelling on business enjoy as comfortable and trouble-free an experience as possible.

**Travel Consultants** – work for both holiday and business travel companies. They advise customers on holiday and travel opportunities and make the bookings for them. This can mean taking straightforward details from a brochure, but it can also cover more complex arrangements. In the case of a specialist travel company offering individually designed holidays to specific areas, the job can involve planning a detailed itinerary across several continents, taking in historic and natural sites of interest and local festivals, and tailored to meet the customer's own personal requirements.

Business travel consultants work for a small number of clients rather than the public. They are responsible for designing complex travel programmes to meet business needs, arranging hotel and conference bookings, and car hire, fitting air flights around hectic business schedules.

**Holiday Representatives** – are based at holiday destinations where they make sure clients enjoy themselves and their holiday runs smoothly. The work includes organising excursions and persuading clients to go on them, working with local hotel and property owners, coach companies and travel agents, checking standards of accommodation, dealing with problems and disputes. Today many companies offer representatives permanent jobs with career development opportunities through movement to UK offices and to different resorts overseas.

**Couriers** – accompany holidaymakers on a trip. This could be a cruise or a special interest holiday visiting classical sites in Italy, or the lochs and glens of Scotland.

They ensure the holiday runs smoothly and iron out problems as they arise, in a similar way to a holiday representative. In addition couriers lead tours, giving background information and a commentary on the areas visited.

**Tourism Officers** – many local authorities in the UK employ tourism officers to encourage people to visit an area. The job involves research into local tourism opportunities, putting strategies in place to encourage visitors, raising awareness of an area through press releases and brochures, organising events and exhibitions, bringing together local organisations and encouraging them to work together.

Salaries in travel and tourism vary enormously. Representatives working in a holiday location are paid around £100 a week rising to more than £200 as they gain experience. They also receive free accommodation and possibly use of a car. In addition they are paid commission on the excursions they sell.

Travel consultants earn between £7,000 and £14,000. Business travel posts are usually better paid than those in the holiday sector.

## Qualities needed

To work in travel or tourism you need to be:

★ A good communicator
★ Genuinely interested in people
★ Tactful, calm and patient – tempers quickly become frayed when arrangements go wrong
★ Flexible in approach and able to think around problems
★ Confident in the use of computers

★ Self-motivated, yet happy to work as part of a team
★ Relaxed and friendly but able to take control
★ Well-organised, able to deal with several issues at the same time
★ Energetic and enthusiastic – helping other people to enjoy themselves can be exhausting.

To work in the travel industry you need exactly the type of skills gained from a media-related degree.

## Getting in

As with many industries today, a career in travel and tourism often means starting at the bottom and learning on the job.

However, there is a growing realisation in travel companies of the need to attract bright, competent people. Several travel companies such as Thomas Cook run international management trainee programmes for graduates. Entry requirements include a degree in any subject plus evidence of an interest in foreign travel in the form of holiday travel, work experience or study abroad.

Tourism officers usually begin their careers as tourism assistants, doing whatever is required in a busy office. To be successful, applicants for such work need to show a strong interest in tourism and knowledge of the area in which they will be working. Tourism officers can go on to apply for tourism director posts.

Jobs are advertised in the national, regional and local press and in specialist publications such as *Marketing Week* and *Leisure Management*.

Cerian Gersbach's interests included both tourism and the media, which is why she chose PR and tourism options for her degree.

## Cerian Gersbach
### PR and Marketing Assistant, British Tourist Association (BTA)

**Degree:** Batchelor of Communications, University of Canberra, Australia

'I finished university and looked for a job in PR, but I always checked the job advertisements for jobs in tourism as well. When I saw a job in Sydney as an information consultant for the British Tourist Association I applied.

'The fact that I'd been to the UK five or so times, travelling and visiting family, helped me to get the job, which involved answering queries from the Australian public and travel trade about coming to the UK. I gave them tips and advice and helped them to make the most of their trip and to stay as long as possible.

'I enjoyed working for the BTA so when, in 2001, I moved to London, I jumped at the chance to work at the Britain Visitor Centre in Regent Street. I work at a corporate level to make sure the centre is used to full advantage.

'Half of all foreign visitors to the UK never leave London and the aim of the centre is to give visitors an idea of what there is to see in other parts of the country and to encourage them to travel further afield.

'We offer a one-stop-shop where people can find out information, book tickets and accommodation and change their money.

'The conference centre and exhibition space at the centre are used by regional tourist boards and other tourist operations to raise awareness among visitors of what is available in areas outside London.

'I help to book and organise these exhibitions and set up press activities to promote them. We've had some great events, including a Taste of Britain month with outdoor cooking demonstrations in Regent Street.

'Another area of my work is giving presentations to foreign trade delegations promoting the UK. I'm lucky that my job combines both my main interests – the media and tourism.'

What can I do with... a media studies degree?

Vanessa Tassetto meets visitors to the UK every day in her job.

### Vanessa Tassetto
### Information Officer, Britain Visitor Centre, London

**Degree:** BA Communication and Culture, University of North London

'I studied tourism in Italy before coming to London to work and study. I speak Italian, English and a little French and my first job in tourism was at the tourist information centre at Victoria Station in London, giving advice and answering queries about the city.

'From there I went to my present job at the Britain Visitor Centre in Regent Street, where we cover the whole of the UK and Ireland and try to encourage people to travel throughout the country.

'I mainly work on the information desk and I find my degree course helps me enormously in my work. As part of my degree I learnt to analyse advertisements, films and television programmes, and this ability to look beyond what people say to what they actually mean is something I use all the time at work.

'After staying in London for a while, people often express the wish to go somewhere quiet. In order to find out what they mean I need to ask some careful questions about their hobbies and interests. For some people it could mean a cottage surrounded by countryside and no neighbours for miles. For others it could be a pleasant town with good pubs and restaurants. If I don't find out exactly what they want, their holiday could be spoilt and they won't come back to the UK.

'I also need to be able to think quickly and laterally. On one occasion a woman came in very distressed. She'd lost her friend, left her luggage at an underground station and forgotten which one, she couldn't remember the name of her hotel and her mobile phone was flat. It took some doing, but with the help of my colleagues we managed to sort out her problems.'

# Education 13

Teaching is an exciting, rewarding career for the right type of person.

The majority of graduates who go into the profession have a degree in a National Curriculum subject, but teaching is still a possibility for those with a media-related degree.

It is the responsibility of the teacher-training provider to look at the contents of a degree course in a non-National Curriculum subject and to decide whether it is sufficiently relevant to the National Curriculum for the applicant to gain a place on a teacher-training course.

Media-related degrees vary enormously in their content and range from the strongly practical to the highly academic, so it is not possible to make any general rule on the eligibility of media degrees. However, in the case of graduates with non-National Curriculum subject degrees, training providers may also take into consideration A-level subjects studied.

If they decide that the degree does not prepare an individual to teach a National Curriculum subject, there are further options available. One is for the graduate to take a short intensive course in the subject to bring his or her knowledge up to the required level. Another is to take a two-year rather than a one-year teacher-training course that includes further study of the subject.

## The job

The majority of schools in the UK are either primary, taking pupils aged 5 to 11 years, or secondary for pupils aged either 11 to 16 years, or 11 to 18 years.

Pupils aged 11 to 16 years in England and Wales follow the National Curriculum, which is made up of the core subjects of English, Maths and Science together with a number of non-core subjects.

Teachers in primary schools are usually responsible for a class of children and teach this class most if not all subjects. In secondary schools teachers specialise in one or perhaps two subjects and teach these to different classes throughout the school. Some areas have a three-tier system with primary, middle and upper schools where middle schools take pupils aged 9 to 12 or 13. The younger years in middle schools are usually run on primary school lines while the older years operate in a similar way to secondary schools.

In addition to making sure pupils learn and develop academically, teachers also have a caring or pastoral role to play, helping to identify pupils who have particular problems and who may be at risk of losing interest in education.

## Qualities needed

Teachers need to have:

★ A liking for children whatever their background and ability
★ An interest in education
★ Enthusiasm for the subject they teach
★ A commitment to helping children achieve their potential
★ Excellent communication skills
★ Flexibility to deal with different situations
★ Patience and determination to manage class behaviour
★ Energy and enthusiasm
★ A sense of humour
★ The ability to work as part of a team, with teachers and other professionals.

The most vital quality needed by teachers is a deep liking for and interest in children. Without this it would be impossible to enjoy the work and do it well. Media graduates who do possess this quality are likely to find their degree studies have helped them to develop many other skills necessary to be a teacher.

## Getting in

In order to train as a teacher, graduates in England and Wales need GCSE passes at grades A to C in English, Maths and Science. In Scotland entry requirements are an H grade in English at C or above, or a National Course award at higher level at C or above in English or Communication, plus an S grade Maths (1–2) or a National Course award at intermediate 2 level in Maths.

The most usual route into teaching for graduates is to take a Post Graduate Certificate in Education (PGCE). Courses are usually full-time for a year and are run by training providers, which are universities, colleges and institutes of higher education across the country. Some part-time courses lasting two years are also available. All PGCE courses include a great deal of time in classrooms gaining practical experience.

Training bursaries of £6,000 are available to graduates taking PGCE courses. In addition, those teaching priority subjects – English (including Drama), Maths, Science, Modern Languages, Design and Technology, Information and Communications Technology and Welsh (in Wales) – are also eligible for a £4,000 taxable 'golden hello'. The Government is currently piloting a scheme where teachers of these priority subjects may also receive help in paying off their student loans.

Flexible training, including training modules taken in the evening and at weekends and by distance learning, is run by some training providers.

There are also employment-based training routes where trainees find a school that is prepared to take them as a trainee. They then follow an individual training plan followed by an independent assessment. If they reach the required standard they become qualified teachers. Such schemes last either one or two years, during which trainees are paid a salary.

To gain a place on a teacher training course, graduates need to show they have a genuine interest in children and education. This should include a significant time spent in schools and working with children in play schemes, summer camps or Brownies, Cubs, drama, sport or musical groups.

Her work in education research has given Kate Lewis an interest in teaching.

### Kate Lewis
**Educational Researcher**

**A-levels:** English, History, Theatre Studies
**Degree:** BA Media Studies, Royal Holloway, University of London

'I work in the English team creating tests to be used in schools by Years 6, 7 and 8 pupils. I research material for the tests, which might be, for example, the biography of a famous person. Then I write the test material and the questions and design a mark scheme.

'I started work with the company four years ago as a holiday job, packing parcels. Six months ago my present job was advertised and I decided to apply.

'It's very interesting work. I'm learning a great deal, receiving excellent training and at the same time I'm being paid a proper salary.

'My job isn't related particularly to my degree, although I do use some of the skills I learnt on my course. I loved my media course, but I wish I'd chosen one that was more practical. My advice to others is to do plenty of research including talking to people on a course to find out what they think about the level of teaching. Some people might have had a brilliant media career but this doesn't mean they can teach what they know and inspire others.

'Whatever your qualification it's important to realise how difficult finding a job in the media is going to be. Not only do you need total commitment to finding work, you also need money and support.

'Jobs as runners are very badly paid and in order to take one and live in an area like London, you need your own money or support from other people. Without this it's just about impossible to manage.

'While I enjoy my job and am learning a great deal from it, it's not what I expected to be doing. However, it has given me an interest in education and I am considering the possibility of teaching media studies in the future.'

Sarah Hamshaw sees a strong link between her degree and her chosen career as a teacher.

## Sarah Hamshaw
### Student Teacher

**A-levels:** English Literature and Language, Psychology, Social Biology
**Degree:** BA English with Media, Falmouth College of Art
**PGCE:** Truro College

Sarah is currently on a PGCE course, training to teach 11- to 18-year-olds. She spends two days a week in college learning about the theory of education and three days in the classroom in supervised teaching situations.

At the beginning of her degree course Sarah was thinking seriously about teaching as a career and at the end of her second year applied for a place on a PGCE course, after visiting a number of different schools and observing classroom situations.

## What can I do with... a media studies degree?

In her words, 'My media degree is a great help in the classroom and every day I use what I've learnt to enhance my teaching.

'For example, one group is studying a short story about a girl running away from home. To support this work, we've seen film clips, listened to a song about a runaway and the group is preparing a Jerry Springer-type show looking at issues arising from the subject.

'Films, videos and television can never take the place of reading, but they can support reading activities. I also use my knowledge of the media to help pupils to look at the impact of television programmes and to appreciate the power of advertising in society.

'At one time teachers taught in their own individual way, which suited some pupils better than others. Today teachers have to adapt their teaching styles to the needs of the pupil. Many classes are mixed ability groups where no one learning style is suited to everyone.

'Teachers must have a flexible approach and go into each lesson with several activities in mind and at least one reserve task in case all else fails.

'Studying the media has helped me to develop a quick response to situations plus the flexibility to change something quickly when it isn't working. It's also helped me to develop my communication skills, which every teacher needs.

'Although most of my time is spent teaching English, which I really enjoy, I am also doing some work with A-level media studies students, which is great.'

# Decisions **14**

If this book has given you some food for thought, now could be the time to act.

First of all, if you are thinking of studying for a media degree, ask yourself why.

Is it because the subject interests you in the same way French or Maths fascinate other people? If so, that's fine. Many media graduates never intend to follow a media career. Their choice of study is purely academic and they go into a wide variety of jobs that usually have no direct relation to their studies, taking with them a range of skills gained from their degree course.

If you are seriously considering a media career, you need to think about the sort of job you want. Do you see yourself appearing on screen as a newscaster or presenter, or working behind the scenes as a lighting technician or camera operator?

It's difficult to answer these questions without direct experience of the industry, which brings you to the next step: finding yourself work placements so you can see for yourself what different jobs involve.

Next come some serious questions. How ambitious and motivated are you? Are you prepared to have very little money, no holidays or new clothes and to put your job before your social life by working weekends and evenings? If the answer is yes, think hard about the route you want to take.

## What can I do with... a media studies degree?

A well chosen media-related degree course can teach you a great deal and help you to make useful contacts, but a great many people with media degrees do not find jobs in the media. Equally many people with no degrees at all or with degrees in completely unrelated subjects can have highly successful media careers.

Ned Parker does not have a media-related qualification.

### Ned Parker
**Associate Producer, Independent Television Production Company**

**A-levels:** Media Studies, Politics, History
**Degree:** BA Politics, Nottingham Trent University

'After taking a degree in politics, I worked in restaurant management and then went travelling.

'When I got back I knew I wanted to get into the media and spent the next nine months working in a restaurant and saving as much money as I could. I joined a networking organisation and went along regularly to meetings in trendy bars to make as many contacts as I could.

'It took time to get anywhere, but eventually I managed to get occasional jobs as a runner on radio, film and television productions, which gave me a broad experience base. The important thing to remember about work experience is that everyone in work knows more than you, so you need to do everything they ask you to do.

'These work experience jobs were usually unpaid, or only paid expenses, so my savings soon disappeared and my debts mounted.

'At the same time my friends were becoming established in various professional fields and were beginning to show signs of affluence. Strangely, the fact that I was so far behind them on the career ladder made me even more determined to keep going.

'Eventually a friend gave me a contact for *London Tonight*. I was offered a chance to shadow the runners for a few days. One left while I was there and I was offered the job – at £12,000 a year. I took it because I'd reached the stage where I was ready to sell my soul for a paid job.

'From there I went on to work experience as a researcher on a live stage show at the Edinburgh Festival. I learnt a great deal there and met a producer who put my name forward with my present company.

'My job varies according to the work we're doing. I work as associate producer and as director. The programmes we produce are varied and include a late night discussion programme for Channel 5 and a documentary on a jazz clarinet player for the BBC.

'Strangely, being a late-comer, with no media degree, tended to work in my favour, possibly because I didn't have idealistic views about working in the media.'

Most of the people profiled in this book have found jobs that they enjoy and certainly nobody feels their studies were a waste of time. Those who did have some reservations about a course tended to be those people who were expecting it to be more focused and more practical with closer links to the industry.

# Planning

Preparation and planning are important, yet life can play awkward tricks. Some of the people profiled in this book planned their careers with care, yet still found that what they thought they wanted, was not for them. Equally, others seemed to wander into a career by chance only to find it fitted like a glove.

# Flexibility

Alongside planning goes flexibility: the ability to accept change and, if necessary, to head in another direction. To do this is not an admission of failure but acceptance of the fact that life is not a straight road, offering only one single opportunity.

Today Paul Bloomfield has a rewarding career as a journalist on a newspaper. Finding the right job wasn't easy for him, but despite disappointments and a depressing amount of time working in a supermarket, he didn't give up.

### Paul Bloomfield
### Reporter, Bury Free Press

NCTJ Newspaper Journalism Course, Harlow College

'I didn't have a clue what I wanted to do after GCSEs so I took a GNVQ in Leisure and Tourism. At the end I knew I didn't want to work in the tourism industry, so I took a BTEC National Diploma in Information Technology. I finished it knowing I didn't want to work in IT either and took a BTEC in Media Studies.

'I had actually found something I enjoyed and a career path seemed to be developing. Suffolk is a rural area and the nearest place to study a media-related HND was 30 miles away from home. I signed up and started the course, but it wasn't for me. I left and took a year out working in a supermarket.

'I'd really enjoyed making videos and so I found a place on a media production degree course, only to find very quickly that despite its name, the course had only a small practical element.

'It was back to the supermarket, with a sinking feeling that I'd never get things right. Then I read about the NCTJ course at Harlow, sent for information, sat the entrance exam and was offered a place. Originally I applied for the magazine journalism course, but after the interview changed to the newspaper course.

'I went back to the supermarket, but this time it was to save as much money as I could. The course lasted nine months and I drove daily to Harlow from Bury St Edmunds because living at home meant I saved money, despite petrol costs.

'We studied law and public affairs and learnt how to write copy for publication. Finally I had found something I really enjoyed. As part of the course I did work experience on my local paper and when the course finished the editor offered me a job.

'I thoroughly enjoy my work. It was worth sticking out for something that was right for me, even if at times it looked as if I was going to spend my entire life working in a supermarket.'

Clare Shute, in contrast to Paul, knew exactly what she wanted to do, gained an impressive first class degree and landed a job in publishing, only to find it did not give her the job satisfaction she wanted. Today she is training to be a police officer with the Surrey Police Force and feels that her media-related degree is a great help in her new career.

## Clare Shute
### Police Constable

**A-levels:** English, Art, History
**Degree:** BSc Media and Communication, Loughborough University

'After leaving university with a first class degree, I worked in sales and advertising with a publishing company for two years and then took a year out to go travelling. On my return I moved to London and worked in sales and marketing with another company specialising in business publications.

'I enjoyed my college course, but I didn't find either of my publishing jobs particularly fulfilling. I spent around 18 months thinking seriously about my future and finally came to the conclusion that I wanted a complete change of job and joined the police.

'I've always been interested in people. I enjoy working in a team and the police is all about teamwork. My degree course was quite theoretical, looking at the effect the media has on society. My final year dissertation looked into the effect a teenage magazine had on different social groups. It involved a lot of time spent interviewing teenagers, asking them questions and listening to what they had to say. The art of interviewing and listening is an important part of police work.

'After studying for a degree I find I can take the academic part of police training in my stride, because I know I am able to remember facts and write an essay.

'I don't for one moment regret studying media. I chose it because the subject interested me and I think it's a great preparation for life in the police.

'In my opinion studying for a degree is about gaining the skills and the confidence to do what you really want with your life.'

# Useful addresses

**15**

## Broadcasting

British Broadcasting Corporation
BBC Recruitment
PO Box 7000
London W1A 6GJ
Tel: 0870 333 1330
Website: www.bbc.co.uk/jobs

British Film Institute
21 Stephen Street
London W1T 1LN
Tel: 020 7255 1444
Website: www.bfi.org.uk

Commercial Radio Companies Association (CRCA)
77 Shaftesbury Avenue
London W1D 5DU
Tel: 020 7306 2603
Website: www.crca.co.uk

FT2 Film and Television Freelance Training
4th Floor
Warwick House
9 Warwick Street
London W1B 5LY
Tel: 020 7734 5141
Website: www.ft2.org.uk

National Media Careers Helpline
08080 300900
Website: www.skillsformedia.com

Scottish Screen
Second Floor

249 West George Street
Glasgow G2 4QE
Tel: 0141 302 1700
Website: www.scottishscreen.com

Skillset
Prospect House
80–110 New Oxford Street
London WC1A 1HB
Tel: 020 7520 5757
Website: www.skillset.org

## Journalism

Broadcast Journalism Training Council
18 Miller's Close
Rippingale
Nr Bourne
Lincolnshire PE10 0TH
Tel: 01778 440025
Website: www.bjtc.org.uk

National Council for the Training of Journalists
Latton Bush Centre
Southern Way
Harlow
Essex CM18 7BL
Tel: 01279 430009
Website: www.nctj.com

Periodicals Training Council
55–56 Lincoln's Inn Fields
London WC2A 3LJ
Tel: 020 7400 7509
Website: www.ppa.co.uk/ptc

Scottish Newspaper Publishers Association
48 Palmerston Place
Edinburgh EH12 5DE
Tel: 0131 220 4353
Website: www.snpa.org.uk

# Publishing

Institute of Publishing
Hamilton Court
Gogmore Lane
Chertsey
Surrey KT16 9AP
Tel: 01932 571932
Website: www.instpublishing.org.uk

London College of Printing
Elephant and Castle
London SE1 6SB
Tel: 020 7514 6514
Website: www.lcp.linst.ac.uk

London School of Publishing and Public Relations
David Game House
69 Notting Hill Gate
London W11 3JS
Tel: 020 7221 3399
Website: www.publishing-school.co.uk or
www.lspr-education.com

Publishers Association
29b Montague Street
London WC1B 5BH
Tel: 020 7691 9191
Website: www.publishers.org.uk

Publishing National Training Organisation
Queen's House
55–56 Lincoln's Inn Fields
London WC2A 3LJ
Tel: 020 7405 0836
Website: www.publishingnto.co.uk

Publishing Training Centre
Book House
45 East Hill
Wandsworth

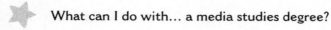

London SW18 2QZ
Tel: 020 8874 2718
Website: www.train4publishing.co.uk

Society for Editors and Proofreaders (SfEP)
Riverbank House
1 Putney Bridge Approach
Fulham
London SW6 3JD
Tel: 020 7736 3278
Website: www.sfep.org.uk

Society of Young Publishers (SYP)
c/o Endeavour House
189 Shaftesbury Avenue
London WC2H 8TJ
Website: www.thesyp.org.uk

## Public Relations

Communication, Advertising and Marketing Education
Foundation (CAM)
Moor Hall
Cookham
Maidenhead
Berkshire SL6 9QH
Tel: 01628 427180
Website: www.camfoundation.com

Institute of Public Relations
The Old Trading House
15 Northburgh Street
London EC1V 0PR
Tel: 020 7253 5151
Website: www.ipr.org.uk

## Marketing

The Chartered Institute of Marketing
Moor Hall

Cookham
Maidenhead
Berkshire SL6 9QH
Tel: 01628 427180
Website: www.cim.co.uk

The Institute of Export
Export House
Minerva Business Park
Lynchwood
Peterborough PE2 6FT
Tel: 01733 404400
Website: www.export.org.uk

## Advertising

Advertising Association
Abford House
15 Wilton Road
London SW1V 1NJ
Tel: 020 7828 4831
Website: www.adassoc.org.uk

The CAM Education Foundation
(see under Public Relations)

Institute of Practitioners in Advertising
44 Belgrave Square
London SW1X 8QS
Tel: 020 7235 7020
Website: www.ipa.co.uk

## Retail

British Retail Consortium
Second Floor
21 Dartmouth Street
London SW1H 9BP
Tel: 020 7854 8900
Website: www.brc.org.uk

British Shops and Stores Association (BSSA)
Middleton House
2 Main Road
Middleton Cheney
Banbury
Oxon OX17 2TN
Tel: 01295 712277
Website: www.british-shops.co.uk

Chartered Institute of Purchasing & Supply
Easton House
Easton on the Hill
Stamford
Lincs PE9 3NZ
Tel: 01780 756777
Website: www.cips.org

Consumer Services Industry Authority
Fraser House
Nether Hall Road
Doncaster DN1 2PH
Tel: 01302 380000
Website: www.csia.net
or www.habia.org.uk

Skillsmart
Second Floor
21 Dartmouth Street
London SW1H 9BP
Tel: 020 7854 8900
Website: www.skillsmart.org.uk

## Sales

The Chartered Institute of Marketing
(see under Marketing)

Institute of Direct Marketing
1 Park Road
Teddington

Middlesex TW11 0AR
Tel: 020 8977 5705
Website: wwwtheidm.com

## Travel and Tourism

British Institute of Innkeeping
Wessex House
80 Park Street
Camberley
Surrey GU15 3PT
Tel: 01276 684449
Website: www.bii.org

Hospitality Training Foundation
Third Floor,
International House
High Street
Ealing
London W5 5DB
Tel: 020 8579 2400
Website: www.htf.org.uk

Hotel and Catering International Management Association
Trinity Court
34 West Street
Sutton
Surrey SM1 1SH
Tel: 020 8661 4900
Website: www.hcima.org.uk

Institute of Professional Sales
(see Chartered Institute of Marketing)

Institute of Sales and Marketing Management
Romeland House
Romeland Hill
St. Albans
Herts AL3 4ET

Tel: 01727 812500
Website: www.ism.co.uk

Institute of Travel and Tourism
Mill Studio
Crane Mead
Ware
Herts
Tel: 08707 707960
Website: www.itt.co.uk

Springboard UK Ltd
3 Denmark Street
London WC2H 8LP
Tel: 020 7497 8654
Website: www.springboarduk.org.uk

## Education

General Teaching Council for Scotland
Clerwood House
96 Chermiston Road
Edinburgh EH12 6UT
Tel: 0131 314 6000
Website: www.gtcs.org.uk

Teacher Training Agency
Portland House
Stag Place
London SW1E 5TT
Tel: 020 7925 3700 or 0845 6000 991
Website: www.canteach.gov.uk

# Whatever careers information you want We've got it!

## (or we know a man who does...)

## Careers-Portal
## The Online Careers Service

- Facts and Figures on all kinds of careers
- HE: Uncovered
- 2000 links to universities, job sites, careers services, employers and more
- Graduate opportunities

**So come online and realise your potential!**

## www.careers-portal.co.uk